The Bahamas

A Family of Islands

Second Edition

Gail Saunders

CARIBBEAN

First published 1988
Reprinted 1990
Second edition 1993

Published by THE MACMILLAN PRESS LTD
London and Basingstoke
Associated companies and representatives in Accra,
Auckland, Delhi, Dublin, Gaborone, Hamburg, Harare,
Hong Kong, Kuala Lumpur, Lagos, Manzini, Melbourne,
Mexico City, Nairobi, New York, Singapore, Tokyo.

ISBN 0 – 333 – 59212 – 3

Printed in Hong Kong

A catalogue record for this book is available from the
British Library.

Cover photographs courtesy of
The Bahamas Tourist Office, UK

Contents

To my Father, Basil North
and
To the memory of my Mother, Audrey North

| Foreword |

Since it was first published, Gail Saunders' book 'The Bahamas – A Family of Islands' has achieved wide popularity not only with visitors but with Bahamians of all ages who use it as a handy, but well-documented, reference to Bahamian life and history.

Her style and depth speak well of her dedication and her love for our country and its people.

On becoming Minister, I had an opportunity to review much information written about The Bahamas, and Dr Saunders' work is still the nonpareil in its class.

On August 19, 1992, when the Free National Movement became the government of The Bahamas, it set as one of its priorities the task of making The Bahamas an environmentally friendly tourist destination sensitive to social issues and ready to release all the creative energies of our people.

We have also set a course of making the names of Exuma, Eleuthera, Bimini, The Abacos, San Salvador and all the other little-known islands in The Bahamas as prominent and recognisable as that of Nassau and Grand Bahama.

The continuing work of Dr Saunders will help this government meet its goals and challenges and we hope that it will inspire other writers and artists to spread the knowledge of the richness and vibrancy of our small but dynamic society.

I again congratulate her on a job well done and wish to assure her and the publishers that works of this kind have my and this government's total support.

Brent Symonette
Minister of Tourism

| Preface |

When Bill Lennox approached me with the idea of writing a guide to The Bahamas, I hesitated. Being a historian and archivist by training, I thought myself unqualified to write such a work. However, after some thought, I realised that my background and also my knowledge of The Bahamas equipped me adequately to attempt such a book.

With the support of my husband, Winston Saunders, my parents, Audrey and Basil North, and Bill Lennox of Macmillan Publishers, I set about a task which has led to much pleasure and knowledge and I am happy to have completed the guide. Although the bulk of the work was written in Nassau, some writing was done in Miami, and in several Family Islands of The Bahamas, including San Salvador, Eleuthera, Harbour Island and Abaco.

The Bahamas: A Family of Islands, after introducing The Bahamas and its people, traces briefly the history of the Commonwealth of the Bahamas. It highlights places of historic interest in Nassau and features three walking tours of the city. New Providence is then explored by car. This section contains information on Paradise Island. Grand Bahama and Freeport are given a separate section, being the second most important tourist centres in The Bahamas. Turning to the Family Islands, brief descriptions are given and tours are made of these intriguing places. The work concludes with sections on 'Night-life' and 'Useful information about The Bahamas'. There is also a list of books for further reading.

I feel confident that this guide will appeal to Bahamians and visitors alike. Read about and explore these marvellous 'Isles of June'. You'll want to know more and you'll return again and again!

Gail Saunders
September, 1987
Nassau

The flamingo is the national bird of The Bahamas (DONN DAVENPORT)

Acknowledgements

Many people have helped to make this book a reality. I am most indebted to Paulene Bastian Smith for her valuable help in preparing the manuscript and Pauline Tait for her cheerful editorial assistance. Thanks are also owed to E. Tommy Thompson and the Ministry of Tourism for supplying tourist information. A special thank you is owed to the Minister of Tourism, Senator the Honourable Brent Symonette, for agreeing to write the Foreword.

A guide such as this would not be complete without photographs. I am grateful to the following for supplying colour slides: Bill Lennox and Michael Bourne of Macmillan, Eileen Fielder and the Counsellors, Peter Ramsey and the Bahamas Information Services, Barry Farrington, Resorts International, Donn Davenport and Gerald Simons. A special thanks goes to Lisa Adderley (Milette), a young and enthusiastic photographer who assisted so ably with the photography.

Certain publications were of invaluable help to me. These included *The Yachtsman's Guide 1987*, the *APA Guide to The Bahamas* and Alison Granfield's *The Bahamas Island by Island*. Certain general histories including Michael Craton's *A History of The Bahamas* and Paul Albury's *Story of The Bahamas* were also useful sources. Sandra Riley's pamphlet on San Salvador was of particular help.

I should like to thank the staff of the Department of Archives for supplying information and for their moral support. Thanks are owed to Don and Kathy Gerace for their hospitality at San Salvador. I am grateful to Gerhard Moog and his family for introducing me to some of the islands of The Bahamas by boat and Mabel Smith and Lorraine Lightbourn for invaluable assistance. I owe a debt of gratitude to my family, especially my parents, Basil and Audrey North, to whom I dedicate this book. Their love, care and support over the years have helped to sustain me. Regretfully my mother died before the book could be published. I am also grateful to my brother Terry, my sister-in-law Bunny, and my mother-in-law Keddie Saunders, for their continued encouragement and support.

My deepest gratitude is owed to my husband, Winston Saunders, for his love, patience and kindness.

The Bahamas

N

NORTH ATLANTIC OCEAN

Walker Cays
Grand Cays
Marsh Harbour
Hope Town
Freeport City GRAND
BAHAMA GREAT ABACO
ISLAND ISLAND
North West
Providence Channel
BIMINI IS
BERRY IS Spanish Dunmore Town
Wells ELEUTHERA ISLAND
Nassau Governor's
Harbour
NEW Rock Sound
Coakley Town PROVIDENCE
ISLAND CAT ISLAND
Tongue of the Ocean The Bight
ANDROS
ISLAND Cockburn Town SAN SALVADOR
Exuma Cays Exuma Sound (Watling I.)
George Rum Cay
Town Port Nelson
GREAT EXUMA IS LONG ISLAND
LITTLE EXUMA IS
Deadman's Cay Clarence Town Samana Cay
Great Bahama Bank (Atwood)
Colonel Hill
Crooked Is Mayaguana
Island
Cay Lobos Rock Ragged
Island Raccoon Cay Acklins
Range Castle I. Island

Mayaguana Passage

LITTLE INAGUA IS

C
U
B
A
Matthew Town
GREAT INAGUA
ISLAND

Scale
0   50   100   150 Miles
0   50   100   150   200 Kilometres

A conch fisherman displays his catch (previous page) (DONN DAVENPORT)

x

| 1 |

'It's better in The Bahamas' – introducing the islands

The archipelago of the Bahamas, comprising some 700 islands, cays and rocks, stretches over 500 miles south-easterly from just off Florida in the north to Cape Haitien in the south. The islands, which are mainly flat, are surrounded by multi-coloured, mainly shallow water in the west, north and south-east. The Lucayan, Taino, called the islands Lucayos. Grand Bahama was called Bahama by the Lucayans, meaning Larger Upper Midlands. By the middle of the 17th century, the islands became known as the Bahama Islands. Some historians believed that it was from the Spanish word *bajamar* meaning shallow sea. There are, however, several deep channels or passages and the colour of the water varies from place to place according to its depth. It is generally turquoise or an almost indescribable greenish colour, especially when hit by the very bright sunlight which is so typical of the region. Astronauts have commented on the unusually beautiful colour of the water.

To add to the beauty of the water, there are miles and miles of white and pink sand beaches. Set behind these are coconut palms, casuarinas or, further inland, pine forests, at least in the northern Bahamas. A temperate climate prevails and there are few sudden changes in temperature. In summer it is rare for the thermometer to rise above 90°F and in winter it seldom falls below 60°F. The humidity, which is high, is compensated by the sea breezes.

Although so near to the North American mainland – you can get to Nassau from Miami in 35 minutes – The Bahamas is different. It has been influenced by America, but is a former British colony. It has a charm of its own, something that is uniquely Bahamian. Life varies from island to island. While Nassau and Freeport are well developed and sophisticated, bustling centres, some of the Family Islands are still largely rural, quiet with small villages.

Strategically placed, The Bahamas can easily be reached from any part of the world. Major American airlines such as American, Delta, and TWA serve Nassau from many major cities in North America.

Additionally, connections to Europe are easily made in nearby Miami; local airlines, such as the national flag-carrier Bahamasair, fly frequently between Nassau and Miami, Freeport and Miami, and West Palm Beach and Fort Lauderdale. Bahamasair also connects Nassau with Freeport and the Family Islands. Numerous luxury liners sail weekly from eastern seaboard ports. Many yachtsmen sail their own boats to The Bahamas or fly in their private planes. There are extensive marina and airstrip facilities in The Bahamas.

Things to do

There are so many things to do that The Bahamas has been called 'Land of adventure'. Besides sunbathing and swimming, there is boating, sailing, fishing, wind-surfing, scuba-diving and para-sailing for the more daring. On land there is tennis, golf, squash, horse-back riding or hiking. You can also shop, enjoy the straw market, and visit the old forts and other historic buildings. There are also the Ardastra Gardens and the Botanical Gardens in Nassau and

A sandy beach on Harbour Island (GAIL SAUNDERS)

Garden of The Groves in Freeport. It is an interesting experience to stroll through the towns and villages on foot in order to appreciate the true atmosphere of the islands.

The best time to go

With such a good climate, it is a pleasure to visit The Bahamas at any time of the year.

The height of the season is between December 15th and Easter. Hotels are usually crowded during these months and it is therefore advisable to book well in advance. Americans flee the frozen northern climes and warm up in The Bahamas. In fact, even during the 'off-season', that is, during the months between Easter and mid-December, The Bahamas is a popular destination and caters to tourists all the year round. There are in fact many added attractions such as Goombay Summer performances during the 'low-season'. The main difference is that rates are lower, often by as much as forty per cent.

The beauty of the sea and land

The beautiful sea which surrounds the islands has already been described. The clarity of the water is fantastic. As there are no rivers in The Bahamas, the water has no silt or sediment. The sea floor is easily seen at 60 feet. The coral formations, underwater plants and fish around the reefs are extremely beautiful. Swimmers and scuba-divers will be thrilled by the warmth of the water.

On the land are many native fruit trees, such as sapodilla, guava, sugar apple and the like. Trees such as the casuarina, the pine, madeira (local mahogany), and a variety of palm trees, including the coconut, add to the beauty. Smaller flowering trees such as the hibiscus, the yellow elder (the national flower of The Bahamas) and oleander give a profusion of colour as does the bougainvillaea plant which creeps over garden walls. From June to September, the poinciana plant, usually a stunning reddish-orange colour, is in bloom and has been the inspiration for many a young artist.

Bird-watchers can also have a field-day in The Bahamas. Many birds fleeing from the colder northern climates migrate to The Bahamas. Inagua, especially, has a variety of Caribbean species. It also contains the largest flamingo colony in the Caribbean, if not the world. The West Indian or roseate flamingo, formerly common on many Bahamian islands, decreased drastically in the early

An aerial view of Bimini and the clear waters surrounding it
(BAHAMAS MINISTRY OF TOURISM)

twentieth century. Because it was in danger of extinction, protective legislation was passed and now The Bahamas National Trust ensures year-round wardening of the flamingo. It is the national bird of The Bahamas. The Bahamas National Trust can arrange guided tours of the preserve. There are also in The Bahamas many different kinds of herons, egrets, ducks, pigeons, gulls, humming-birds, woodpeckers, mockingbirds and thrashers just to name a few. There are owls and even parrots, at least in Abaco and Inagua. Birds are protected by legislation governing the shooting season and also by National Parks in Inagua, the Exumas, the Abacos, Grand Bahama and Conception Island, which are operated by The Bahamas National Trust.

Sports

Local Bahamians enjoy sport tremendously. Any morning or afternoon, joggers, walkers, swimmers, tennis players, footballers or cricketers can be seen practising their sports. The islands abound with facilities for tourists, especially in the large resorts such as Nassau and Freeport. There are about 100 tennis courts in the Nassau/Cable Beach/Paradise Island area alone, and about 200 in total for all the islands. Additionally, there are twelve championship golf courses, most of which are open to visitors on payment of green fees. Some of the resort courses are free to guests. In the Family Islands, there are eighteen-hole golf courses at the Treasure Cay Beach Hotel in Abaco and at the Cotton Bay Club on Eleuthera. Both hotels have tennis courts as well.

In Nassau there is a diving school for budding scuba-divers. Famous for its lovely reefs is Andros. At the island's Small Hope Bay Lodge, instructors take divers to the barrier reef which runs along Andros's eastern shore. There is also snorkelling in the shallower

Wind-surfing off Nassau on a breezy day (LISA ADDERLEY)

water, reef fishing, sailing and wind-surfing. San Salvador, the first landfall of Columbus, is also renowned for its beautiful reefs.

In Nassau you can experience the serenity and beauty of under-water without being a scuba-diver. At Hartley's Undersea Wonderland Ltd, beginners can walk on the bottom of the ocean without even getting their heads wet. The underwater walk is supervised by Christopher Hartley, an experienced diver. It is educational, exciting and an ideal outing for families. No experience is needed in either diving or swimming.

Catamaran cruises through Nassau's picturesque harbour and along the north side of Paradise Island are available from the Prince George's Wharf. They last for three hours and the visitor can sightsee to the strumming of a calypso band while sipping a cool drink. Time is always made for a swim at one of the most beautiful beaches in The Bahamas.

There are also all-day 'shipwreck' cruises where you spend a day on an island relaxing in a hammock, exploring beaches, snorkelling and swimming. Food is cooked on an open fire – it is a fabulous all-day 'Out Island' picnic.

Excursions are also available twice a week to Treasure Island from Nassau Harbour Club. On the island you can swim, sunbathe, snorkel, explore or just laze about. Snorkelling equipment is supplied free and lunch is included in the price of the excursion. Bar service is available on the island. This tour is operated by Island Excursions Ltd.

Fishing is also popular in The Bahamas. There are few fishing grounds that can equal those in the islands. Game-fishing is particularly popular at Bimini. For those who are not into fishing, boating by either sail or power is equally exciting. In The Bahamas, cruising, especially through the Exumas or the Abacos, is a beautiful experience. Hundreds of miles of clear calm water await the adventurer, who can also drop anchor off hilly harbours or white sand beaches.

Hunting is another Bahamian sport. Pigeons, coots, doves and ducks are plentiful. The shooting season is limited, however, usually starting in September and ending at the end of March. Big game hunters can track wild boar at Andros or at Abaco.

Variety in accommodation

There is a variety of accommodation in The Bahamas ranging from the most luxurious hotels on Paradise Island and Cable Beach, and on some of the Family Islands, to smaller guest-houses. During the high or winter season rates are quite high, ranging from about $40.00 a day for a basic, clean room at a small guest-house to $110.00 for a room in a first class hotel. But do not be deterred by the relatively high rates; there are package tours which include hotel rates and air fares which make for an economical holiday. Call your travel agent for the latest information. The Ministry of Tourism also has a list of the more modest guest-houses.

| 2 |
Introducing the Bahamian people

Bahamians, who number about 250,000, are mainly of African descent – 85% being black and 15% being white; some are mixed. The white population are descended mainly from the early English settlers who arrived on Eleuthera in 1648. Many can also trace their roots back to the American Loyalists who after 1783 fled the newly independent States with their slaves. A large proportion of the black population had forebears who were enslaved. Minority groups include Greeks, Chinese, Syrians, Lebanese and Haitians. Despite the proximity to the United States, Bahamians have maintained their own identity.

The mainly thin and infertile soil soon led to the decline of the plantation. Emancipation in 1834 brought the plantation era to a close. The population, both black and white, survived for over a hundred years on a variety of industries, the most important being farming and fishing. Sponge-fishing was to sustain The Bahamas' economy for three-quarters of a century. Sisal, salt-raking, pineapple and tomato growing were other important industries. The struggle to survive built up a resilience in the Bahamian character. The islands also prospered because of their close proximity to the United States. Bahamians did not hesitate in taking advantage of the American Civil War when Nassau was used as an entrepôt by the Confederacy, or during Prohibition, when Bahamians became involved with the bootleggers.

Bahamians are a dynamic, independent and friendly people with a sense of humour. Their friendliness is evident in the Ministry of Tourism's 'People to People' programme. Visitors who write or call at the Ministry of Tourism can arrange to meet Bahamians, who usually invite them to their homes for a meal or show them a bit of The Bahamas.

The vitality and dynamism of Bahamians can be seen in the amount of energy that is put into every aspect of life. Bahamians love to celebrate. A celebration can be arranged in days or even a few hours. Some events, though, such as weddings, are planned months in advance. Not only is the church ceremony meticulously arranged, but so also is the reception which follows at either a hotel or the home of the bride's parents.

Funerals, although very solemn affairs, are well-planned and can end in a get-together of the family and close friends of the deceased, a gathering which usually ends in a party. Wakes, which are celebrations of the passing of the loved ones, are usually held before the funeral. At wakes, chanting and singing are common as are eating and drinking!

Religion is an integral part of Bahamian life. Even the smallest village has a church or two. The largest denomination is Baptist, the faith having been introduced to the island by a runaway American slave, Sambo Scriven. The Anglican (or Episcopalian) Church, originally the Established church in The Bahamas, boasts the next greatest number of followers. Next are the Roman Catholics and then the Methodists. The Church of God also has a large following as does the Pentecostal Church. There are also smaller sects such as Presbyterians (which was also Established until 1869), Jehovah's Witnesses, Seventh Day Adventists, Christian Scientists and Muslims. The Baptists and Church of God offer much freedom of worship. Bahamians are also attracted to the emotional display manifested in the singing, chanting and clapping during the services. Some members 'get-the-spirit', or God-inspired inspiration during the services.

Music is important to Bahamians. No Bahamian can stand still if there is a drum beating or a calypso playing. Calypso, of West Indian origin, has a subtle rhythm and satirical lyrics which often comment on some aspect of West Indian life. Goombay is music of the drums and originated in Africa.

Every week during the summer there is a Goombay evening in Nassau and at the Mall in Freeport. During Goombay there is a Junkanoo Parade and the Jump-in dance.

The Jump-in dance resembles the Fire Dance and Ring Play. Each is held upon the formation of a ring. Participants stand in a circle around one or more dancers. There is clapping, singing and sometimes drum rhythms. Solo dances take place in the circle. A solo dancer performs in the centre of the ring and after dancing for a short period chooses one person, usually of the opposite sex. The sequence is repeated. The dance is lively and rhythmic.

9

Junkanoo – a pan-African celebration (GAIL SAUNDERS)

Junkanoo is a pan-African celebration. It is the soul of the Bahamian! It can be traced back to slavery. Slaves were given three days off and during that time they celebrated by having a 'grand dance'. Today Junkanoo is celebrated in the early hours of Boxing Day and New Year's Day on Bay, Frederick, Shirley, and Parliament Streets in Nassau. It is also celebrated on a smaller scale in Freeport and on some of the other Family Islands. At minutes to three a.m. in Nassau, a throbbing rhythm from cowbells, drums, whistles and bugles is heard in the distance. It gradually gets nearer and nearer, culminating in a heightened rhythm which cannot be resisted. The pulsating music makes even the most staid sway with the rhythm. The wonderful, throbbing music is made by the 'Junkanoos', who are dressed in a variety of costumes. Large groups are now formed, their fringed costumes made of brightly coloured crêpe paper usually designed to fit a particular theme. Each group also has a music section. Junkanoo is spectacular and should not be missed. During Goombay Summer a much smaller version of the Christmas Junkanoo can be seen.

Also to be seen during Goombay Summer is 'Beating the Retreat' by the Royal Bahamas Police Band. This is a spectacular display of marching and counter-marching in a series of figurative movements.

At the same time, music is played and the bulges and drum-tapping make everyone want to join in the dazzling spectacle.

Other displays by the Royal Bahamas Police Band are held on commemorative and special occasions such as the opening of each session of the Supreme Court, the opening of the Legislature, the Independence Day Anniversary Parades in New Providence and Grand Bahama, the annual Remembrance Day Parade and at military funerals.

Bahamian drama and art have come into their own. There is a repertory season at the Dundas Centre for the Performing Arts on Mackey Street. This includes serious drama, musicals and dancing. Various drama groups also present musicals and drama in the off-season. Works of art can be seen at the various galleries including R. Brent Malone's studio, 'The Temple' on East Bay Street and Marlborough Antiques on Marlborough Street. The Central Bank sponsors an annual art competition for aspiring local artists in December.

In spite of its British past, its African heritage and its proximity to North America, The Bahamas has managed to maintain a uniqueness of its own. There are English customs that have survived, for example the Changing of the Guard and the adherence to British legal traditions. There are also a number of African continuities such as Junkanoo, the Jump-in and Fire dance, and Obeah. There are also strong links with America – Bahamians sometimes do their grocery shopping in Miami and the local supermarkets are packed with American goods. However, despite the strong links with the colonial past and the accessibility of the US dollar and its cities, something truly Bahamian remains.

| 3 |
A colourful history

The geology

Millions of years ago, The Bahamas land area was much larger than it is today. The most recent Ice Age over a period of thousands of years caused the oceans to rise and slowly engulf the limestone islands. Because of the warm water temperature, coral thrives and The Bahamas is known for its reefs and coral atolls.

The first inhabitants

The Siboney, Meso-Indians, who migrated into the Greater Antilles, were probably The Bahamas' original inhabitants. However, when Columbus 'discovered' the islands in 1492, he found Lucayans and called them 'Indians'. They were in fact Arawak-speaking people related to those neo-Indian Arawaks in the larger Caribbean Islands and practising a Tainan culture. The Arawaks had originally come from the South American mainland. Being peaceful by nature they were forced northwards by the more warlike Caribs. It is believed that they arrived in The Bahamas between AD 500 and 600, being settled from Cuba and Hispaniola. The Lucayans, as the Arawaks came to be known in the Bahamas, had no written language – only a spoken one. Quite a number of Arawak words such as avocado, iguana, cannibal and potato have survived. From archaeological research and the study of Lucayan artefacts, we can imagine what the Lucayans were like and how they lived.

From Columbus' descriptions, it seemed that the Lucayans were a brown-skinned people with coarse black hair. Their faces were broad with foreheads being flattened in childhood to add distinction to their looks and to shield them from enemy blows. They wore scant clothing, and adored ornaments. Some had tattoo marks. They were peace-loving, and a favourite pastime was the singing and dancing which they called *arieto*. They also played a ball game, something like the modern-day volley-ball, which they called *batos*. Like their Arawak cousins to the south, they probably smoked tobacco in y-shaped pipes. Lucayans lived in rectangular or circular huts which were sparsely furnished. They usually slept in hammocks and lived in small villages which were headed by chiefs called *caciques*. Lucayans mainly farmed and fished for survival. For food, they grew maize, yams, sweet potato and cassava. They hunted a small mammal called the *hutia* or agouti, and sometimes snared birds. The sea yielded much of their food. Fish, turtle and conch were popular features of their diet.

Spiritually, the Arawaks had a highly developed form of religion, believing in two supreme gods. They also had a belief in spirits or *zemis* which lived in trees. Some of the carved images of *zemis* survived and have been excavated.

Columbus and the discovery of the islands

It was the gentle Lucayans who greeted Christopher Columbus at Guanahani on the historic 12 October 1492. Columbus, sponsored and financed by Queen Isabella and King Ferdinand of Spain, captaining the 100-ton *Santa Maria* and accompanied by the smaller *Nina* and *Pinta*, left Spain on 3 August 1492 and undertook perhaps

Columbus lands at 'Guanahani', believed to be the present-day San Salvador, in 1492 (THE MANSELL COLLECTION)

the most historic thirty-three-day voyage across the Atlantic Ocean. In search of Cathay and the East, Christopher Columbus and his crew finally landed at an island in The Bahamas which the Lucayans called Guanahani. It is almost certain that it was the present-day San Salvador (a theory well argued by S.E. Morrison in 1941). However, there has been much debate about this subject. Some scholars, including Eris Moncur, place the landing on Cat Island, others on Caicos Island, Rum Cay and Mayaguana. Recent research by Joseph Judge, former Senior Editor of the *National Geographic Magazine*, argues for Samana Cay, but this has been largely discredited by scholars. The landfall controversy will continue. Suffice it to say

The plaque outside The House of Assembly in Nassau which commemorates the formal annexation of The Bahamas
(MICHAEL BOURNE)

that Columbus *did* land initially in the Bahamas on 12 October 1492 – a date well known to school children. Moreover, 12 October (Discovery Day) is observed every year as a public holiday. The landfall in The Bahamas opened up the West and began a new era in the history of the world.

After exploring San Salvador, Columbus took several Lucayans with him as guides and explored several other Bahamian islands including Rum Cay, Long Island, Crooked Island and the Ragged Islands.

The Spaniards, after the 'discovery' of the 'New World', settled on the larger and richer Caribbean islands of Hispaniola and Cuba, where precious metals were to be found – not so in The Bahamas. The only interest to the Spaniards of The Bahamas was its population. Between 1500-1520 the Spaniards deported almost the entire population of Lucayans to be used as slaves in the gold and silver mines and plantations, and as divers in pearl fisheries set up by the new settlers. When Ponce de Leon visited The Bahamas in 1513 in his vain search for the miraculous fountain of youth, he could only find a single old crone in all of the islands he visited.

1629 grant of the islands

During the time between the depopulation of the islands and the next settlement, many Elizabethan seamen such as Richard Grenville, John White, Sir Francis Drake and Sir John Hawkins navigated in Bahamian waters, but none of the islands was formally appropriated until Charles I (1625 – 1649) included them in a grant of proprietary rights on the American mainland to Sir Robert Heath, the English Attorney-General and an ardent Loyalist. Although no settlement was made, 30 October 1629 stands as the date of the formal annexation of The Bahamas and is commemorated on a plaque outside the House of Assembly in Nassau.

The Eleutherian Adventurers

The Bahama Islands remained virtually unsettled until 1648 in which year the Eleutherian Adventurers, led by Captain William Sayle, former Governor of Bermuda, landed at Cigateo or Segatto, renamed 'Eleutheria' from the Greek word for freedom. In fact, the Adventurers left Bermuda and England searching for religious freedom. We can never be sure where the settlers landed after being shipwrecked. One theory is that it might have been Governor's

A typical house in Spanish Wells, North Eleuthera (GAIL SAUNDERS)

Harbour. We do know that William Sayle and a Captain Butler had a violent argument and this caused a split. It is believed that Sayle took most of the settlers to Spanish Wells and Harbour Island; the others settled at another part of Eleuthera. However a local historian has argued (very plausibly) that New Providence was the first island settled. Otherwise, how did it get so far ahead of Eleuthera population-wise? Perhaps when the dispute arose aboard ship during this voyage from Bermuda to The Bahamas, Sayle put the dissidents ashore on New Providence, and the other group sailed to North Eleuthera. It is believed that they sheltered in Preacher's Cave and may have used it as a church and burial ground for some years.

Wherever they settled, the colonists had a hard time of it. They lived at near starvation level, exporting braziletto (a dye-wood) and ambergris (a secretion of the sperm whale used in making soap), and depended largely on the salvage from wrecks. An elaborate constitution called the Articles of the Adventurers was drawn up providing for an elective senate, a governor and council, but it seems

16

that no effective government existed in the new colony and in 1670 the Bahamas Islands were granted to the six Lords Proprietors.

The Lords Proprietors

By a Charter of 1670, Charles II (1660-1685) granted The Bahamas to six of the Lords Proprietors of the Carolinas giving them the right to make laws and appoint governors. The Governors were to see that an assembly was elected. As far as we know the Governors failed dismally in their task. The forty-eight-year period of Proprietary Government was confusing and tumultuous; the Governors were most inefficient, corrupt or ineffectual. Indeed three Governors were dismissed, two seized and shipped abroad by the inhabitants, three never arrived, one was murdered by the Spaniards, two just left for England and one never took up the governorship. The period was one of 'pirates and plunder', lawlessness and defencelessness, poverty and wrecking, absentee landlords and inefficient governors. The Spaniards attacked in 1702. New Providence was sacked in 1703 by a combined force of French and Spaniards and again in 1705 and 1706 by the Spaniards alone. The last Spanish attack on New Providence took place in 1782.

Among the pirates who frequented Bahamian shores were Benjamin Hornigold, Major Stede Bonnet and two female pirates, Mary Read and Ann Bonney. Edward Teach, alias Blackbeard, probably left the greatest mark – there are a tower, a well and a steak tavern named in his memory. In the Nassau Public Library there is a picture of a huge silk cotton tree once supposedly situated on the Eastern Parade which was known as Blackbeard's tree. Under this tree Blackbeard is alleged to have held court and had parties. The story goes that the tree was later cut down and sent to England to be made into little jewellery boxes, which were popular in those days.

Woodes Rogers – first Royal Governor 1718

After a long period of unstable rule the government of the Bahama Islands was finally vested in the Crown, and on 6 February 1718 Captain Woodes Rogers, an ex-privateer renowned for his round-the-world voyage, became the first Royal Governor.

Rogers on the one hand aimed to suppress the pirates but also offered pardons to those who reformed. Those who refused were executed or chased out of New Providence. He had Fort Nassau, then the only fort on New Providence, repaired and several guns mounted. The citizens were organised into a militia of three companies to defend the town and others were put to work cleaning the roads and clearing the bush around Nassau, 'so that it began to have the appearance of a civilised place'. During the period of his first governorship (1718-1721) Woodes Rogers appointed government officials such as the governor's secretary. Unfortunately most of Rogers' men died in an epidemic and, when no help came from England after many requests, Rogers left The Bahamas in 1721, having spent his fortune. For his efforts he was sent to a debtors' prison on his return to England.

Governor George Phenney was appointed in his place. Phenney did try to secure a meeting of an Assembly. Council meetings were held and are in fact recorded from 1718. Phenney, however, fell into disfavour because of the corrupt practices of his wife. She monopolised trade and sold 'Rum by the pint and Biscuits by the Half Ryal' (three penny-worth).

It was therefore not until Rogers' second period of office as Governor in 1729 that steps were taken to call a General Assembly

The lighthouse at the entrance to Nassau Harbour (LISA ADDERLEY)

which first met on 29 September 1729. The Assembly comprised twenty-four members who were elected and no less than twelve Acts were passed.

It is from this time that the government of The Bahamas can be said to have been formally constituted.

Shipwrecking and illegal trade

After Rogers' death in 1732 the colonists turned to shipwrecking and profited from illegal trade between the French and northern colonial ports which passed through The Bahamas. Many ships passing through Bahamian waters were often blown off course during hurricanes on to Bahamian reefs. False beacons brought hundreds of vessels to their doom as the colonists rushed out to help themselves to the cargo. Shipwrecking in the eighteenth and nineteenth centuries became an 'industry' and it is said that the Government issued licences to 'wrecking families' who shared their findings with New Providence officials; even parsons indulged. The industry flourished until the establishment of Nassau Harbour in 1816. Others were to follow in the 1850s, 1860s and 1870s.

The American Revolutionary War, the Loyalists, slavery and emancipation

The American Revolutionary War broke out in 1776 between those who wanted independence from Great Britain and the British, including some Americans, who were still loyal to the Crown. This war was to have a significant effect on the development of The Bahamas.

In the early part of the war American rebels attacked The Bahamas and captured it easily. They dismantled the forts and took all the gunpowder and ammunition that could be found, carrying off the Governor as a hostage.

Later during the war, in 1782, Nassau capitulated to the Spaniards for the last time. The Spanish occupation lasted a little over a year. New Providence was brilliantly retaken for the Crown in 1783 by Colonel Andrew Deveaux, an officer of South Carolina, who, with 'a handful of ragged Militia and five privateers', deceived the Spaniards as to their force and strength, drove them from Fort Montagu and captured the island of New Providence. Deveaux did not know that the recent Treaty of Versailles in January 1783 had restored The Bahamas to Britain.

**Fort Fincastle, built during Lord Dunmore's governorship to
help defend New Providence** (MICHAEL BOURNE)

Loyalists

In 1783, after the end of the American Revolutionary War, many
people who were still loyal to the British Crown, encouraged by
land grants, began to migrate to The Bahamas from New York,
Florida, South Carolina, Virginia and Georgia. From 1784 to 1785
about six thousand Loyalists and their slaves migrated to The
Bahamas. Population-wise, before their influx there were only about
four thousand people in the whole Colony with just under twice
as many negroes as whites. While the white population doubled,
the black trebled. The newcomers brought ten to a hundred slaves
each and set up plantations on New Providence and the Out Islands.
The chief commercial crop grown on plantations was cotton. The
first three years were productive ones, but by 1788 the industry
began to fail. The chenille or red bug attacked the crops and by 1800
the cultivation of cotton was seriously affected. The decline in

cotton meant the decline of the plantation system and the new prosperity.

Slavery

The Bahamas had a substantial slave population, one that was mainly creole, i.e. born in the New World. Most lived in small units. There were no very large sugar plantations in The Bahamas as there were in the southern Caribbean. As cotton declined, the slaves turned more and more to subsistence agriculture. Many worked as domestics and mariners in the town of Nassau. In spite of the economic conditions, there were cases of cruelty and even some revolts.

The slaves who came with the Loyalists were joined by thousands of liberated Africans who were captured by the British navy, freed and put ashore in The Bahamas. Villages such as Adelaide and Carmichael in New Providence were settled by such 'free Negroes' between 1808 and 1860. By the latter date, the main pattern of the population had been laid down. The majority of Bahamians were of African descent with a minority being descended from the early English settlers and Loyalists. A few minority groups, for example the Greeks, Chinese, Jews and Syrians, came later.

Emancipation

The Empancipation Act in August 1834, which abolished slavery in all British colonies, gave limited freedom to the ex-slaves. The Act incorporated the apprenticeship period during which time the ex-slaves worked for their ex-masters for board and lodging or a salary. It was supposed to be a time of adjustment but was quite irrelevant for The Bahamas. By this time, with the impending collapse of the plantation system, most slave owners were very poor. They still resisted abolition however, although many slaves in The Bahamas were freed before 1834. Slavery was finally abolished in The Bahamas on 7 August 1838; this signalled the final collapse of the plantation system. The destiny of The Bahamas now lay in the hands of free men. Following emancipation, the general condition of the West Indies was one of poverty and disillusionment. Poverty was rampant; paid employment was not readily available. The ex-slaves and the ex-masters struggled to exist. Many took to subsistence farming. Others remained on the land of their former owners and worked it on the share system. There was hardly any circulation of money in the Out Islands and many communities were tied by a system of payment by truck, i.e. payment in kind.

American Civil War and the blockade
It was not until the outbreak of the American Civil War in 1861 that The Bahamas again became temporarily prosperous. President Lincoln's blockade of the southern ports at the beginning of the war meant that they had no way of getting their cotton out and their supplies, including ammunition, in Nassau, which was fairly near to the two most important southern ports, Charleston and Wilmington, became the rendezvous and neutral port that the gunrunners and cotton traders used. Nassau became prosperous over-night. The harbour was packed with ships and the Royal Victoria Hotel, built between 1859 and 1861, became the headquarters of the blockade runners. However, the boom was shortlived and not everyone profited in any case. When the war ended in 1865, the Colony slumped into depression.

Attempts at local industries
Attempts were made in the latter part of the nineteenth century to build up home industries such as sponges, sisal, pineapples, and citrus fruit. From the late nineteenth century until 1938, sponging was the major item in the Bahamian economy. In that year a mysterious fungus hit the sponge beds and the value of exports rapidly declined.

Twentieth century

First World War 1914-1918
For the most part, The Bahamas remained a remote corner of the Empire during the First World War. Some Bahamians were exposed however – about 670 Bahamians went to war. The Bahamas also supplied fruit, vegetables, clothing and medical equipment to countries suffering from the effects of the war.

The Bahamas suffered little effect from the war. The tourist trade did not collapse until the winter season of 1916 – 1917. After the United States entered the war, The Bahamas suffered food shortages. When the war ended in 1918 the soldiers returned to a little changed Bahamas. The economy was in decline. The passing of the Volstead

Act by the United States' Congress in December 1919 was to be more important to The Bahamas in its effects than the events of 1914-1918.

Prohibition

The United States passed a law in 1919 prohibiting the import or manufacture of liquor in the United States. Nassau again profited by becoming the port from which the 'rum runners' loaded up their ships with liquor from England and Scotland and smuggled it into the States using swift boats.

A number of Bahamians made fortunes during this time, mainly by selling liquor to American bootleggers who in turn smuggled it into the thirsty United States. Not many Bahamians actually 'ran' the liquor themselves. When the Volstead Act was repealed in 1932, The Bahamas' economy again slumped and the general outlook became for the most part gloomy.

Sir Harry Oakes

Into the gloomy Bahamian economy of 1934 arrived Sir Harry Oakes, a Canadian multi-millionaire. He bought up much land in New Providence and the Out Islands, including Oakes Field, which he paved. It was the first aerodrome in The Bahamas, and its construction gave work to many unemployed Bahamians at this time.

Second World War 1939-1945

Just over a thousand Bahamians volunteered for service in the Second World War and fourteen actually lost their lives in active service. The Bahamas, moreover, contributed generously in financial terms to the war effort and also sent twenty shipments of useful articles collected by the War Materials Committee. The Bahamas itself suffered little from the war; it was never a theatre of war. The economy, especially the tourist trade, which was depressed in 1939, enjoyed a boom in the season of 1940-1941. Bahamians hardly knew what rationing was – it was not until 1942 that there was limited rationing. Many Bahamians found work on the two new Air Force bases situated at Oakes and Windsor Fields. The Bahamas became a training base for the United States Army Air Corps and the Royal Air Force. It was also a staging-post on the trans-Atlantic ferry service and a base for ocean patrol and service and air-sea rescue work during the anti-submarine campaign in the Caribbean and west Atlantic.

Duke of Windsor appointed Governor

In August 1940, the Duke of Windsor, formerly King Edward VIII, was appointed Governor of The Bahamas, a post which he occupied until 1945. He had given up the throne to marry American divorcée, Mrs Wallis Simpson, 'the woman he loved'. Blake Higgs, better known as 'Blind Blake' wrote a song about the former King:'It was love, love alone, caused King Edward to leave the throne'.

The Duke of Windsor's most lasting work was the formation of an Out Island and Economic Committee which attempted to increase the productivity of Out Island farmers. He also founded a much-needed infant welfare clinic on Blue Hill Road.

Three happy, healthy Bahamian children (MICHAEL BOURNE)

Riot of 1942

During the governorship of the Duke of Windsor, serious riots occured over a wage dispute. On 1 June 1942, thousands of labourers working on 'The Project' (a large installation being built under the 'Land-lease' arrangement) at very low wages gathered 'Over-the-Hill' and stormed down 'Burma Road'. They descended on Bay Street, breaking windows and looting shops. A company of Scottish troops (Cameron Highlanders) were called out, the Riot Act was read and martial law was declared. In dispersing the crowds and maintaining order during the next few days, five persons died as a result of the riot and of the curfew. Many more were injured.

The Project

Between 1943 and the mid-1960s, thousands of Bahamians, mainly men, went on 'The Project' in the United States for periods of between six to nine months at a time. There, they were employed mainly on farms picking crops. They earned much more than they could at home and part of their salary was deducted and sent to the Post Office Savings Bank in Nassau. Working on The Project exposed Bahamians to cultural differences and blatant discrimination in the United States.

Murder of Sir Harry Oakes

Another event which made international headlines at this time was the mysterious and still unsolved murder of Sir Harry Oakes. Oakes' son-in-law, Alfred de Marigny, was charged with the murder but was acquitted by a Bahamian jury. He was however deported from the Colony.

Tourism, finance, Freeport

Tourism

Tourism started on a minor scale in the late nineteenth century. In 1873, the best tourist year before the twentieth century, five hundred winter visitors came to Nassau. In the late 1890s, with the advent of a regular steamship connection between Nassau and the

The entrance to The International Bazaar in Freeport, Grand Bahama (overleaf) (MICHAEL BOURNE)

25

United States and Flagler's New Hotel Colonial, northerners began to holiday in The Bahamas. In 1914 the Development Board was established for the promotion of tourism and soon, under the guidance of the late Sir Stafford Sands, began to advertise all over the world. In 1949, 32,018 tourists visited The Bahamas; by 1968 over a million came and the three million mark was achieved in 1986. Tourism has become our major industry.

Finance

The Bahamas also depends to a large extent on investors, having no well-developed natural resources of its own except for the tourist trade and some light industries. Nassau has become a banking centre; in 1946 there was only one bank, the Royal Bank of Canada, but now there are over three hundred banks and trust companies.

Freeport

In 1955, The Bahamas Government granted Wallace Groves' Bahama Port Authority 50,000 acres of land, with an option over a further 50,000, with the agreement that the company would build a great freeport and industrial centre. Concessions were granted by an Act of the same year, guaranteeing freedom from taxation of income, capital gains, real estate or personal property until 1985 and from all customs and excise duties (except on goods for personal use) until 2054, and also freedom from immigration restrictions. An act of 1970 nullified the latter.

By 1961 Freeport had fifty miles of road and hundreds of buildings including a hospital, a clinic, a modern school, supermarkets and a model airport terminal which is now an international airport. It has developed tremendously since that time, becoming the second most important tourist centre in The Bahamas. It has two gambling casinos and has developed light industries such as the Syntex Factory, a cement plant and a multi-million-dollar oil refinery – BORCO.

Political parties and reform

The Progressive Liberal Party

The first Bahamian political party, the Progressive Liberal Party (PLP), dates back to 1953 and the meeting between Mr William

Cartwright, *Bahamian Review Magazine* publisher, H.M. Taylor, the junior member of the House of Assembly for Cat Island, and Cyril Stevenson.

Messrs Cartwright, Stevenson and Taylor spearheaded the movement. Soon to join the party was a young lawyer Mr Lynden Oscar Pindling, destined to become the leader and The Bahamas' first black Prime Minister. He was entrusted with the preparation of the party's platform for the 1956 election.

The 1956 Election, and formation of the
United Bahamian Party

In the 1956 General Election, the PLP, dedicated to reform and fighting corrupt practices, obtained six seats. By its united front, it provoked the formation of a second political party, the United Bahamian Party (UBP), in 1958. This party represented the majority of those elected, comprising mainly white Bay Street merchants.

General Strike 1958

The General Strike of January 1958, led by Randol Fawkes, Labour leader and former PLP member, temporarily affected The Bahamas' economy but its longer term effects were favourable. Bahamian problems had come to the fore, and the Colonial Office responded by sending its then Secretary of State for the Colonies, Mr Alan Lennox-Boyd, to investigate. Important electoral changes were recommended and the property qualifications and plural vote were abolished. Nassau was given four more seats in the House of Assembly, which were all won by PLP candidates in the by-election of 1960. Also in that year an Act was passed giving women the right to vote and to sit in the Legislature. The election in November 1962, in which women voted for the first time, was disappointing for the PLP; the UBP were returned with an increased majority.

New Constitution, 1963

A New Constitution, instituting ministerial government, came into force on 7 January 1964. The Cabinet was established and consisted of the Premier (in 1969 renamed Prime Minister, under the Pindling Administration), Sir Roland Symonette, and not less than eight other ministers and took over the general direction and control of the government, becoming collectively responsible to the legislature. The legislature was bicameral and consisted of an Upper House, the

Senate, comprising sixteen members, and a Lower House, the House of Assembly, comprising thirty-eight members.

Change of government

On 10 January 1967 the Progressive Liberal Party (PLP), who represented the majority black population, was elected into power replacing the previous United Bahamian Party (UBP) government or 'the Bay Street Boys'. Mr Lynden O. Pindling became the first black Prime Minister of The Bahamas. The 'quiet revolution' had begun.

The majority was slim and, in the next year, the death of a member forced another General Election. On 10 April 1968 the Progressive Liberal Party swept into power winning twenty-eight of the thirty-eight seats.

In November 1971 the Free National Movement was formed by a merger of the Free-PLP and the UBP to form the major opposition party. A General Election was held on 19 September 1972, the main issue being that of Independence, while the Free National Movement, although in favour of eventual Independence, thought that it should be delayed. The Progressive Liberal Party was returned to power by a landslide majority, winning twenty-nine of the thirty-eight seats in the Lower House. On 19 August, 1992, the Free National Movement, led by Mr Hubert Ingraham, swept into power winning thirty-one of the forty-nine seats in the House of Assembly.

Independence

The white paper on Independence was laid on the floor of the new House when it met on 18 October 1972.

Talks were held between the Government, Opposition and British Government in London in December 1972 to discuss the Constitution for an Independent Bahamas. The date for Independence was set for 10 July 1973. Except for a threatened secessionist movement by Abaco, which had some foreign support, The Bahamas gained independence peacefully. Bahamians witnessed week-long celebrations which culminated with a cultural historical pageant: the lowering of the Union Jack and the raising of the new Bahamian flag; the singing of the new Bahamian National Anthem, 'March on Bahamaland'; and the handing over of the Constitutional

Policeman on guard duty at Government House (MICHAEL BOURNE)

Instruments on 10 July. His Royal Highness, Charles, Prince of Wales, presided for the Queen. Sir Milo Butler, who had recently been knighted by Queen Elizabeth, became the first Bahamian Governor-General, taking up office in August 1973. The Hon. Lynden O. Pindling became the first Prime Minister of an Independent Bahamas.

Post Independence

Since 1973, the Commonwealth of The Bahamas, under a Progressive Liberal Party Government until August 1992 when the FNM took over, has made considerable progress in developing health care, education, sport, tourism, finance and business in general. Numerous social and economic measures have been taken in order to raise the standard of living for the majority of the people. Many schools have been built and, in 1974, the College of The Bahamas, offering tertiary education, was established. Housing those in the lower income bracket has been a priority of the Government. Efforts have also been made to establish and keep The Bahamas' reputation as a 'Zurich of The West'. In 1974 the Central Bank was established and four years later The Bahamas Development Bank, which provides finance for the small businessman, was opened.

During the last decade The Bahamas has also established itself in the international community. It is a member of the United Nations, OAS, UNESCO, CARICOM and the Commonwealth. In October 1985 it hosted the prestigious Commonwealth Heads of Government Conference in Nassau. Nearly all of the Commonwealth's Prime Ministers attended. Her Majesty the Queen and His Royal Highness Prince Philip, who stayed on the Royal Yacht *Britannia*, were also in Nassau. In 1992, the Quincentennial year or the 500th anniversary of the landfall of Christopher Columbus in the Bahamas and the 'New World', The Bahamas hosted the CARICOM Foreign Ministers and the 22nd meeting of the OAS's General Assembly (both in May) and the Commonwealth Parliamentary Association meeting in October.

| 4 |

New Providence –
an exciting island

Exploring by car

Going west

Starting at **Nassau Street** drive west along West Bay Street past Xavier's College, a privately run Roman Catholic School, on the left and the Western Esplanade and public beach on the right. Immediately after Xavier's College and the **Road Traffic Inspection Centre** turn left and follow the road to the Gun Powder Storage and **Fort Charlotte**. The latter was built by Lord Dunmore who was Governor of The Bahamas between 1787 and 1796. Named in honour of the wife of King George III, the main (that is the eastern) portion was completed in 1789, while the middle bastion, Fort Stanley, and the western section, Fort D'Arcy, were added at a later date. As you will see, the walls of the fort were cut out of limestone. A dry moat surrounded the fort and was spanned by a wooden bridge on the northern side. In fact the fort never fired a shot in anger. It stands as a historical site surrounded by about 100 acres which Dunmore reserved as public lands. There is a magnificent view of the harbour from the fort. Also to be seen is **Arawak Cay**, a man-made island which was built by the Government of The Bahamas in the late 1960s. On the island is a base which receives fresh water barged in from Andros Island. A recent development is **Coral World** on **Silver Cay** which is connected to Arawak Cay by a bridge.

Coral World includes a spectacular underwater observatory tower. Part of the tower is submerged to a depth of 20 feet below the surface of the water and from it one can see natural coral reefs and marine life in its natural habitat through the numerous clear windows. There is also a bar and two observatory terraces from which to view the ocean, Paradise Island and Cable Beach. The tower rises 100 feet above the water. Silver Cay itself has been converted into a marine park where man-made streams, waterfalls, coral reefs, shark tanks, a marine garden aquarium, along with many

New Providence

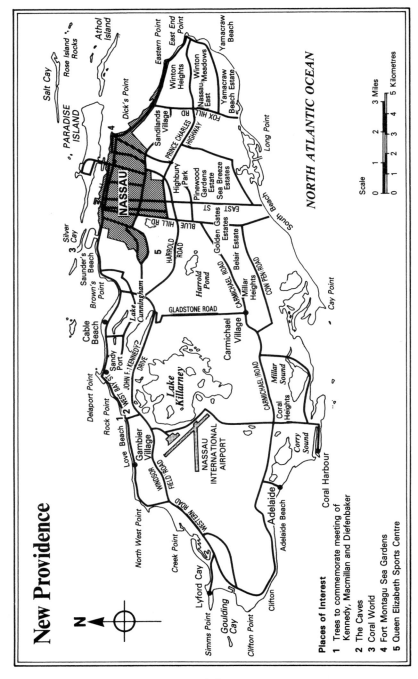

Places of Interest

1 Trees to commemorate meeting of Kennedy, Macmillan and Diefenbaker
2 The Caves
3 Coral World
4 Fort Montagu Sea Gardens
5 Queen Elizabeth Sports Centre

NORTH ATLANTIC OCEAN

Scale

0   1   2   3 Miles
0 1 2 3 4 5 Kilometres

34

other exhibits, can be seen. Also featured on Arawak Cay is a Coral World Hotel which is small, having 22 ocean-front rooms each with a private pool. A seaside restaurant is also an attractive feature of the island. Be prepared to park on Arawak Cay and take a bus ride across the bridge to visit Coral World, Bahamas. It is open every day. There is an admission fee.

Leaving Coral World, turn west on West Bay Street and then left into Chippingham Road. Not far from the main street are the **Nassau Botanic Gardens** which comprise about eighteen acres of tropical

The Observatory Tower at Coral World (LISA ADDERLEY)

gardens with a variety of plants, trees and flowers. The gardens, which were recently redeveloped and rededicated, are open daily to the public. Near the Botanic Gardens are the **Ardastra Gardens and zoo** which are open daily from 9 a.m. to 5 p.m. Guided tours begin at 10:30 a.m. and 3:30 p.m. There are three flamingo shows daily at 11:00 a.m., 2:00 p.m. and 4:00 p.m. The Ardastra Gardens are best known for their world-famous marching flamingoes, which have performed since the 1950s. Here the flamingo, the national bird of The Bahamas, is kept in captivity and trained. You can stand a few feet away from the birds as they march by. The flamingoes have been featured in the *National Geographic Magazine*, on many TV shows and in numerous fashion magazines.

Also featured in the almost five-acre gardens are parrots from tropical regions and The Bahamas, monkeys from South America, lemurs from Madagascar, and iguanas from The Bahamas. There are also peacocks and over 300 other birds, mammals and reptiles.

Leaving the Ardastra Gardens, re-enter Bay Street and go west. After passing a small shopping centre, private homes and apartments, you will soon see **Saunders Beach**, a popular bathing place for

The national flower of The Bahamas, the yellow elder (G. W. LENNOX)

36

Bahamians and tourists alike. The approach to Saunders Beach at twilight is lovely. Lofty casuarinas line the beach which lies opposite the Silver Cay Club Apartments and **Tony Roma's A Place For Ribs**. From Saunders Beach there is a scenic view of the bridge and observatory tower at Coral World.

Near to Saunders Beach is the **Grove**, once a sisal plantation. This area was developed by G.R. Baxter and H.G. Christie in the 1920s as a subdivision known as Vista Marina. It is a popular suburb, being only ten minutes from Nassau. Adjacent to it is **Highland Park** which is a sought-after residential area.

Continuing on Bay Street you will pass **Brown's Point**, more popularly known as **Go-Slow Bend**. As you drive past, adjacent to the western coast, there is a lovely view of the Cable Beach Resort Hotels, sometimes called the 'Western Riviera'. Cable Beach was so named because the first cable communication between Nassau and Jupiter, Florida was laid in the area in 1892. From the early 1950s, the area began to be developed as a tourist resort. Today, just past **Goodman's Bay**, there is a complex of hotels, some of them owned by the Government. Just recently the old **Emerald Beach Hotel**, the first to be constructed on the strip, was demolished to make way for the **Radisson Cable Beach Casino and Golf Resort** and the **Crystal Palace Hotel** which has five towers and was built by the Carnival Cruise Ship Lines Company. The Radisson Cable Beach Casino and Golf Resort, which was built by the Hotel Corporation, was the site of the Commonwealth Heads of Government meeting in 1985. Included in the amenities of the Crystal Palace Hotel are a gambling casino and a shopping mall which offers a wide variety of goods. There are also tennis courts, squash and racquet ball courts and other sporting facilities. The **Ambassador Beach Hotel** is also owned by the Hotel Corporation. It stands on the site of Westbourne, the former house of the late Sir Harry Oakes who was mysteriously murdered there in 1943. The first class **Nassau Beach Hotel**, which is run by the Wyndham Company, is next to the Crystal Palace.

Continuing on West Bay Street, you pass a residential section and soon approach another superb hotel, **The Royal Bahamian**, (formerly known as the Balmoral Beach Hotel). It has many luxurious facilities including a health spa, swimming pool and tennis courts.

The Crystal Palace Hotel at Cable Beach (overleaf) (MICHAEL BOURNE)

Other smaller hotels, including **Casuarinas Hotel**, dot the coastline.

Continuing further along West Bay Street, passing many beautiful, and some quite luxurious properties, you approach **Delaporte Point** and beach. A recent development, **Sandy Port**, has made the area into a Venice-like resort and residential area. A bridge links the new area to the beach. Nearby, to the west, is the small village of Delaporte, formerly a plantation owned by Joseph Thompson. There are several restaurants and bars where visitors can purchase drinks and native dishes such as conch salad.

Continuing on West Bay Street, you soon reach **Rock Point** where a part of the movie *Thunderball* was filmed. After Rock Point, the road hugs the coastline and the views of the sea are magnificent. The next point of interest is **The Caves** which developed naturally out of soft limestone. There is an inscription above the caves which commemorates the arrival of the first member of the Royal Family, Prince Alfred, Duke of Edinburgh, who landed at New Providence on 3 December 1861. Just west of The Caves is Blake Road which leads to John F. Kennedy Drive and to Nassau's International Airport. Several trees, planted by John F. Kennedy, Harold Macmillan and John Diefenbaker, stand at the intersection of Blake Road and West Bay Streets to commemorate their meeting in Nassau in 1962. The spot is known as **Conference Corner**.

A little beyond the caves is **Orange Hill**, once owned by G.R. Baxter, the developer of the Grove Estate. It now boasts a small hotel and restaurant and overlooks a fine bathing beach which runs along the coast for about half a mile. Opposite the beach, on quite hilly ground, some luxurious houses have been built. The coast soon becomes rocky as you approach **Gambier Village**, originally settled by liberated Africans captured on the high seas by the Royal Navy after the abolition of slavery in 1807. Some of the settlers of Gambier also came from the *Creole*, on which a mutiny by slaves took place in 1841 in Bahamian waters, near Abaco. One of the mutineers who settled there was an Elizah Morris. In the old days the villagers lived mainly from farming, the products of which were sold in the Nassau Market. Modern Gambier has its own churches, a school and several petty shops. Many of its inhabitants work in varied industries including tourism.

Further west along the coast is **Love Beach**, named after a once

Deserted stretches of beach can still be found on New Providence
(MICHAEL BOURNE)

prominent family of that name. There are a number of private houses and apartment complexes in this scenic area. Love Beach itself has a fine swimming area. West of it is **Old Fort**, which was once a part of an estate, Charlotteville. An ancient house remains on the site and overlooks Old Fort Beach, perhaps the best beach on the island of New Providence. The next place of note is **Lightbourn's Creek** which also has some fine swimming waters. After passing the old Waterloo Estate, once owned by the former Attorney-General and Loyalist, William Wylly, we approach **Lyford Cay**. The latter, named after Loyalist William Lyford, was developed on a small scale by H.G. Christie in the early 1950s. Later, in the 1960s, Canadian financier E.P. Taylor spent millions of dollars turning the once remote and thickly wooded area into an exclusive resort for the wealthy. The Lyford Cay Club and Hotel has some of the finest tourist facilities. It also boasts of a very well-kept eighteen-hole golf course, numerous tennis courts and also promotes water sports such as scuba-diving, water-skiing and swimming. Lyford Cay is home for many celebrities, including theatre producers, best-seller authors and famous actors. Its gates are protected by a rigid security system, so someone must expect you before you will be allowed to enter the gates. Just before the gate there is a shopping complex which includes boutiques, a dry-cleaning outlet, pharmacies, a furniture shop, and an art gallery. There is also a gas-station.

Near to Lyford Cay is a more modest development called **Mount Pleasant** where professional Bahamians and some of the people who work at Lyford Cay have made their homes. Some also are employed by a nearby hotel known as the **Ramada South Ocean Golf and Beach Resort**. This resort, which has 195 beach front and garden view guest rooms, offers golf on its very fine eighteen-hole course, as well as tennis and swimming. Located on part of the golf course near the road are the ruins of an old plantation.

Continuing on the western road you soon come to the western tip of New Providence, known as **Clifton Pier**, or **Clifton Point**. In the late eighteenth and nineteenth centuries William Wylly had a large plantation at Clifton where provisions were raised for the slaves. It was also used as a landing place for passenger ships in rough weather. Today, Clifton is the site of the Bahamas Electricity Corporation's main plant. It also serves as a gasoline storage depot.

In 1987, the Commonwealth Brewery opened a factory at Clifton. Clifton can also boast of being the site for the film *Jaws 1987* which starred Michael Caine. Locally-born actor Cedric Scott co-starred in the film.

If you continue along the coast you will pass the South Ocean Hotel's golf course and beach. Eastwards is **Adelaide Village** at **South West Bay**. The village was founded in 1831 when the then Governor, Sir James Carmichael Smyth, settled about 157 liberated Africans who were never slaves, but who had been captured by the Royal Navy on the Portuguese ship the *Rosa* and freed. The Government supplied the liberated Africans with basic supplies encouraging them to build their own homes at the village. A school and church were later established. Even up to the early 1960s a few thatched huts made of tabby-stone, typical of the original houses, could be seen. Today, the village has modern amenities such as electricity, telephones and good roads. It still, however, has an aura of serenity and quaintness about it. The beach, especially at sunset, is beautiful.

Travelling east on Adelaide Road you soon come to the **Coral**

Harbour-side stalls (MICHAEL BOURNE)

43

Harbour roundabout. Coral Harbour is a residential area with man-made canals and also accommodates the **Bahamas Defence Force Base**.

Joining the main road, now Carmichael Road, and travelling east, you pass sparsely-populated and partially-wooded areas. Along Carmichael Road is the road to **Bacardi and Company Limited.** The Bacardi Company moved much of its business to The Bahamas after the Cuban Revolution in 1959. At the Gladstone Road and Carmichael Road junction there is the **Carmichael Bible Church**, a foodstore and a drug store. It is really the site of the Carmichael Village (although little can be seen of the original village) known as **Headquarters**. It was the earliest liberated African village established by the Governor, Sir James Carmichael Smyth. Some of the Africans who had settled at Carmichael left in 1825 to form a settlement near the town of Nassau in order to be near the Nassau Market. The area is now known as **Grant's Town**. Many Carmichael settlers found work in the town. The population of Carmichael Village itself dwindled from about 797 in 1830 to 215 by 1837.

By turning north into **Gladstone Road** you can cross the ridge on to **John F. Kennedy Drive** which runs along the shore of one of the two lakes in New Providence, **Lake Killarney**.

Continuing along Carmichael Road the route passes Millar's Heights, Flamingo Gardens, Belair and Golden Gates Estates. Near the latter is **Nola's Bake Crabs** which sells a Bahamian delicacy, spicy baked crab, which is made from local crab meat, bread crumbs and spices, all baked in the original shell. A new highway, Milo Butler Drive, connects Harold and Carmichael Road, opposite Faith Avenue.

At the end of Carmichael Road turn north on **Balliou Hill** or **Blue Hill Road**. On the southern side is the **Golden Gates Shopping Centre**. Passing over the hill and by the **Bahamas Electricity Power Station** and the **Family Guardian Insurance Company**, you will see the **Independence Shopping Centre** on the left. Continuing on Balliou Hill Road you will pass the **A.F. Adderley Senior High School** and the **Yellow Elder Primary**. Further north is the **Bahamas Electricity Administration Building** and the site of the **National Insurance Building**, formerly known as **Jumbey Village**.

At the corner of Balliou Hill Road and Wulff Road is **St Barnabas Anglican Church**. Further north the road passes through **Bain Town** which is located to the west of Grant's Town. The two towns

44

have merged and the area is popularly known as 'Over-the-Hill'. Originally a part of a 140-acre land grant to Susannah Weatherspoon, Bain Town was bordered on the east by Blue Hill Road, on the north by South Street, on the south by Poinciana Drive and on the west by Nassau Street. The area was probably named after Charles H. Bain, a black businessman who bought the area after 1840. Bain divided the land into allotments, selling them to liberated Africans and former slaves. The southern part of Bain Town was popularly known as **Contabutta**, and is said to have been settled by the Congo people who were looked down upon by the other settlers or Yorubas of Bain and Grant's Town.

Just east of Bain Town is Grant's Town, first laid out by Governor Sir Lewis Grant and the Surveyor-General, John J. Burnside, between 1820 and 1829. It includes the area bordered on the east by East Street, west by Balliou Hill Road, north by Cockburn and Lees Streets and south by the Blue Hills. As mentioned earlier, Grant's Town is seething with life. It contains 'no end' of petty shops where everything is sold. Men playing checkers, dominoes and *warri* (an African game) can still be seen in the Over-the-Hill area.

Some of the most distinguished and prominent Bahamians, including Deputy Prime Minister Orville Turnquest, came from Over-the-Hill. The former Prime Minister, Sir Lynden O. Pindling, hails from **East Street**, one of the major thoroughfares of Over-the-Hill. Once the site of a market, and previously a heavily wooded area, Over-the-Hill contains many native restaurants, bars, clubs, churches and offices. It is the home of **St Agnes Anglican Church**, on the corner of Cockburn Street and Balliou Hill Road. First consecrated in 1848, the present church dates back to 1868. Not too far from St Agnes is **Wesley Methodist Church**, established in 1847 to serve the southern Methodists. Other prominent churches in the area include **The Church of God of Prophecy** on East Street and the **Church of God**.

Turn west at Balliou Hill Road and Meeting Street. Along Meeting Street is the **Bethel Baptist Church**, which stands on the site of a very early foundation. The original Bethel Meeting House was probably built at the beginning of the nineteenth century. It was a small wooden structure which was demolished by the 1866 hurricane. The present structure, most of which was built this century, contains a small part of the church that was rebuilt in 1869. Near to Bethel Baptist Church, on the opposite side of the street,

45

is **St John's Baptist Church**, founded in about 1835 by Prince William, a freed slave from South Carolina. Because these churches were originally 'meeting houses', the street soon became known as **Meeting Street**, a name that is still used today. At the western end of Meeting Street, return to Nassau Street, the starting place of 'going west' by car.

Going east

Starting at **Victoria Avenue**, travel east along Shirley Street. Just past School Lane is **The Tribune** office, established in 1903 by the Dupuch Family. It is still a family-run evening newspaper. Opposite the Tribune is the Ministry of Education, formerly St Andrew's School and originally the **Collins Estates**. The main structure was built by Ralph G. Collins in the late 1920s. Mr Collins was then a very prominent businessman and politician. Acquiring the building and a portion of the land in 1950, St Andrew's School Limited converted it into a school. It was purchased by the Government in 1970 and has been used as the Ministry of Education since June 1972.

Just past the Ministry of Education is **Collins Avenue**, formerly a part of the Collins Estate. On the western corner of Collins Avenue and Shirley Street is the **Chamber of Commerce** head office and on the other corner is **Doctors' Hospital**, formerly Rassin Hospital, which was developed by a former RAF doctor, Meyer Rassin.

About half a mile going east on Shirley Street is **St Matthew's Anglican Church**, originally known as the eastern church as it was considered 'beyond the skirts of the East extremity of the town ...'. Built between 1800 and 1802 by a Loyalist, Joseph Eve, St Matthew's is the oldest church building in The Bahamas. It is a simple rectangular shape with the nave and aisles under one roof. At the western end of the church there is an octagonal tower and steeple, the latter erected in 1816. At the bottom of the tower is the baptistry and west door. The church was enlarged in 1887 and has been extensively renovated in recent years. The original stained glass window was erected in memory of Bishop Venables (1863-1876), the second Bishop of Nassau.

Just to the east of St Matthew's, on the southern side of Shirley Street, is **Ebenezer Methodist Church**. Originally known as a 'meeting place' for Methodist followers in East Nassau, the original wooden building was constructed in 1802. It was later destroyed by a hurricane and the foundation stone of the present building was

The Paradise Island Bridge (G. W. LENNOX)

laid in 1839, the building being opened for worship in 1841. There is an interesting cemetery behind and in front of the church.

Continuing east on Shirley Street you soon come to **Mackey Street**, a main artery which connects **Paradise Island** and New Providence by a bridge. If you turn south into Mackey Street you will pass the **Public Records Office/Department of Archives** on the left-hand side. Established in 1971, the Public Records Office is the final repository for the permanent Records and Archives of the Government. There are also records from schools, churches, public corporations and private families. Many records are on microfilm, especially those which have been copied from repositories abroad. Archival records in the Public Records Office contain the fundamental information about the history of the country and are a treasure trove for historians and other researchers, including the genealogist.

There is also a small lending library, the **Eastern Public Library**, which occupies the top storey of one of the Department of Archives' buildings.

Next to the Department of Archives is the **Salvation Army's** main headquarters and the Central Corps. Established in The Bahamas in 1931, the Salvation Army has a school for the blind and many programmes for the poor. There is also a Grant's Town Corps and the Samuel and Cornelius Williams Centre for the Aged on Meadow Street in Bain Town. They also have programmes on the Family Islands.

Further south on Mackey Street is the **Ranfurly Home for Children**, a centre for orphaned and deserted children. Opposite is the **Learning Resources Unit**, a part of the Ministry of Education which services teachers with its multi-media library and broadcast programmes.

Opposite the Learning Resources Unit is the **Dundas Centre for the Performing Arts** which began as a Civic Centre for training domestics. It now runs a repertory season annually between January and May. It features serious drama, musicals and also produced the first Bahamian Opera *Our Boys* with the music written by Cleophas Adderley Jr and the libretto by Winston Saunders and Philip Burrows. Various groups such as the Nassau Players, the Nassau Operatic Society, the University Players and The Bahamas Drama Circle are an integral part of the theatre and have representatives

Sailing boats in Montagu Bay (LISA ADDERLEY)

on the Board. The groups perform there before and after the repertory season.

Retrace your route to the roundabout which leads to **Paradise Island** (see below), turn right and continue eastwards along East Bay Street passing the **Yacht Haven**, the **Poop Deck** and the **Pilot House Hotel** on the southern side. The latter is a modestly-priced hotel with good restaurants and a swimming pool. It is good for hosting small conferences and also a favourite with businessmen and spring-break students.

Continue eastward past a beautiful office building originally intended for Banco Ambrosiano which now houses **Bank America Trust and Banking Corporation** and several other offices. After passing some quaint residences, some overlooking the water and others inland and hidden by foliage, you will come to **Club Waterloo** on the southern side. This is a popular night-spot for the 'younger set'. Opposite is the **Nassau Yacht Club**, which dates back to the 1930s. It is popular with sailors and has produced Olympic champions such as Durward Knowles and the late Cecil Cooke. Around the curve continuing on East Bay Street is the entrance to Fort Montagu beach and also **Fort Montagu**. The latter was built between 1741 and 1742 by Peter Henry Bruce who was appointed engineer by the British Government to restore fortifications in The Bahamas. Bruce completely rebuilt Fort Nassau, the site of which is now occupied by the British Colonial, and constructed the new Fort Montagu and an adjoining sea battery called Bladen's Battery. These two together were to guard the eastern entrance to Nassau harbour.

Leaving the Fort, rejoin East Bay Street passing the once popular Montagu Hotel built in 1926 and which has been closed for some years. Turn into Shirley Street and then almost immediately left into **Village Road** which runs from north to south connecting Shirley and Bay Street with Bernard, Wulff and Soldier Roads. On Village Road is **Queen's College**, a co-educational Methodist High School established in 1890 which moved from Charlotte Street in the early 1960s. Opposite the school is **The Retreat**, the headquarters of **The Bahamas National Trust**. The Retreat sits in a large eleven-acre estate once owned by Arthur and Margaret Langlois. Between them they collected some of the rarest palms in the world. Tours are conducted through the gardens daily. Village Road also boasts a squash racquets club, a bowling alley, a plant nursery and a large food store. As it branches off into Bernard Road there are several small shopping centres, including restaurants.

Return to East Bay Street and the now derelict Montagu Hotel, and turn east, past the **Royal Nassau Sailing Club** which is an exclusive club catering to yachtsmen and those interested in the sea. Continuing eastwards you will pass luxurious and palatial homes which sit opposite the foreshore. Nearly opposite **Blair**, once owned by a single family, now a well-kept subdivision, is a small settled area, known as **Dicks Point**. Shortly after Dicks Point is **The Hermitage**, originally built by Lord Dunmore as a country estate, and now the residence of the Roman Catholic Bishop of Nassau.

It is a most scenic drive along the Eastern Road. Homes on the sea side are mostly walled-in with some type of creeping colourful plant peeking over. Some homes resemble the Bermuda-style homes which were so beautifully painted by Winslow Homer in the late nineteenth century.

Still going east past **High Vista** which leads into a subdivision and, shortly afterwards, **Fox Hill Road**, turn south into Fox Hill Road past **St Anne's Anglican Church**, first constructed in 1740. The present church was built later between 1867 and 1870. Next door to the church is **St Anne's School** which is co-educational for children of both primary and secondary levels. It is operated by the Anglican Diocese.

Further along Fox Hill Road, at the junction with Bernard Road, there is a roundabout which is in the heart of **Fox Hill**, named after Samuel Fox, a former slave who owned land in the area. Some years later, the then Chief Justice of The Bahamas, Robert Sandilands, bought about 1200 acres in the Fox Hill area. In 1840 he laid out a village and made nearly a hundred grants of land varying from one to ten acres. Liberated Africans received grants and paid in money or labour. They called the settlement **Sandilands** after their benefactor. Until the 1960s, Fox Hill was a remote, heavily wooded area which produced fruits and vegetables, some of which were sold in the Nassau Market. Some Fox Hill women walked from their village down to the Nassau Market with trays gracefully balanced on their heads.

Sandilands Village was later divided into four towns, **Joshua, Congo, Nango** and **Burnside Town**. Some are still referred to by these names today. The area still has some wooded areas. It boasts many churches, petty shops, a public library, a fire station and a school. A community centre which includes the library and Post Office was dedicated in early 1988. The area also accommodates the Boys and Girls Industrial Schools, Sandilands Rehabilitation Hospital for the mentally ill, the Geriatrics Hospital and the Prison. At the centre of the village is **Freedom Park** opened in 1967. The residents of the area celebrate Emancipation Day on the first Monday in August and Fox Hill Day on the second Tuesday in that month. The custom which originated in the nineteenth century commemorates freedom from slavery.

Along Bernard Road, which is one of the main arteries leading into Fox Hill, are **St Augustine's Monastery** and **St Augustine's College**. The latter is a co-educational high school run by the Roman Catholic Diocese. The complex was established by the Benedictines from St John's, Collegeville, Minnesota. The monastery was designed by Father Jerome Hawkes who later went to live at Cat Island where he built a small shrine on top of Mount Alvernia in which he lived as a hermit. His design for the monastery included rooms opening on to cloisters with an arched stone roof to match the cloisters.

Return to the junction of East Bay Street and Fox Hill Road and continue east. You soon pass **Blackbeard's Tower**, an ancient structure built as a fortification, probably in the eighteenth or nineteenth century. The hilly strategic site is believed to have been used by the notorious Edward Teach, also known as Blackbeard, who frequented the Bahamian archipelago during the sixteenth and seventeeth centuries. He is reputed to have used the site, which has a view of the eastern harbour, as a look-out.

Continue east past **Camperdown**, once heavily wooded, now quite a built-up residential area. Near to Camperdown is **Winton Heights**, once a large plantation known as 'Lookout'. On **Winton Highway** there are many fine homes with marvellous views of the eastern harbour, and **Rose Island**, a small cay which runs almost parallel to the eastern end of New Providence. Nearly half-way up on the ridge are the remains of **Fort Winton**, a small fortification built by Lord Dunmore. Inland from Winton Heights is Winton Meadows, a more modern subdivision boasting many palatial homes.

Return to East Bay Street and continue east, hugging the coast. **McPherson's Bend** was named for a resident who, legend has it, parked his car there every night to enjoy the cool breezes and the view! Continue along the coast past **Yamacraw Beach** which is very near to **St Andrew's School**, a private co-educational

A good example of one of the older houses in New Providence. This style of architecture is rapidly disappearing (MICHAEL BOURNE)

institution established in the 1940s. New subdivisions, Port New Providence and Sea Pointe, have been developed nearby. Soon afterwards you will pass the southern entrance to **Nassau East**, a subdivision established in the 1960s which adjoins Nassau Village. Part of the Government's housing project, **Elizabeth Estates** is to be seen before reaching **Her Majesty's Prison**.

Turn right at the Prison and pass the various Government institutions mentioned earlier, then, at the junction, turn left to **Prince Charles Drive**. Here there are various business complexes which are developing in a once residential area, as well as a number of subdivisions off the highway including **Sea Breeze Estates, Pinewood Gardens** and **Highbury Park**. Prince Charles Drive goes into **Robinson Road** on which there are several Government schools and business houses. At the junction of Robinson Road and East Street turn right or north and continue in a northerly direction through the 'Over-the-Hill' district into town. East Street runs from the south to the north coast.

There are many side streets and other areas into which you may wish to drive. New Providence is an island with contrasting landscapes. It has fine white-sand beaches on its north coast, pleasant suburbs in its eastern, western and southern areas and a bustling but quaint town – Nassau – on its northern shore. Some of the neo-colonial architecture has been lost, but enough remains to remind us of our colourful history. Nassau is surely the most attractive city in the anglophone West Indies.

Paradise Island – glamour and serenity

History

The island resort which is today known locally and internationally as Paradise Island was originally named Hog Island. The late Paul Albury, the noted Bahamian Historian, tells the island's story in his very readable *Paradise Island Story*. For many years, Hog Island was undeveloped. Old-timers rowed over to the island to explore, to swim or to ride breakers on the inviting beaches. From early times the island invited those seeking pleasure. In the late eighteenth century there was a 'Banqueting House' where picnics were held.

In the late nineteenth century, tourists began to be attracted to the island. Local Bahamians began to offer boat rides to the island and provided changing rooms. Fruit was offered, the most famous being the oranges which, after being freshly picked, were put on sticks and served to the guests. Some proprietors began to encourage tourists further by adding attractions such as sack races, candly pulls, bicycle rides and dancing lessons. The site of most of this activity, Saratoga Beach, has become known as **Paradise Beach**.

Hog Island's reputation also boasts a flirtation with Swedish industrialist, Dr Axel Wenner-Gren. He arrived in Nassau in his yacht the *Southern Cross* in 1939, the year that the Second World War erupted. Being attracted to Hog Island, he bought the Lynch Estate and dredged Burnside's pond, re-christening it Paradise Lake. Wenner-Gren also constructed canals linking the lake with Nassau Harbour and the ocean to the north. Rumour has it that Wenner-Gren built the canal for a fleet of German submarines and a Nazi U-boat base. He also renovated the Lynch Estate calling it Shangri-La.

Paradise Island

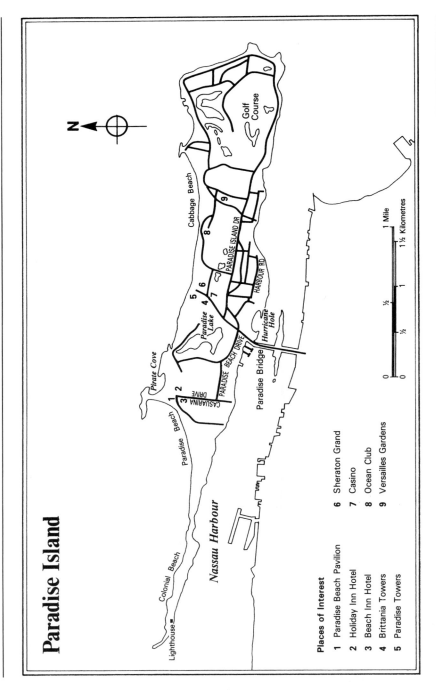

Places of Interest

1 Paradise Beach Pavilion
2 Holiday Inn Hotel
3 Beach Inn Hotel
4 Brittania Towers
5 Paradise Towers

6 Sheraton Grand
7 Casino
8 Ocean Club
9 Versailles Gardens

Huntington Hartford

Much later, in 1961, the year of his death, Wenner-Gren sold his Hog Island estate and holdings to Huntington Hartford, heir to the Atlantic and Pacific Tea Company fortune. Hartford had the island renamed **Paradise** in 1962 and soon built the plush and exclusive 52-room **Ocean Club** which is still open today. The hotel retains its old world charm. Its Georgian-style architecture, inner courtyard, world-renowned tennis courts, which attract the likes of John McEnroe, Vitas Gerulaitis and others, and its fine swimming pool attract guests from all over the globe. Besides enjoying the quiet but active atmosphere of the hotel, guests can wander in the grounds and view the **Versailles Gardens** and **Cloisters** for themselves.

Huntington Hartford imported the medieval cloisters from a monastery near Lourdes in France. The Cloisters, which were bought in pieces, were rebuilt over a year and today provide a beautiful scene and the serenity that is lacking in some of the modern

One of the many attractive golf courses in The Bahamas
(G. W. LENNOX)

amenities of the island. Brides, grooms and their parties often take their special photographs at the Cloisters.

The **Versailles Gardens** lead up to the Cloisters. Consisting of a series of about seven terraces, the gardens boast a sundial which is mounted on a twelfth century gothic pedestal, flanked by two fountains. There is also a twelfth century statue of Hercules and, on another level, statues of David Livingstone and Franklin D. Roosevelt. Also to be found in the gardens are marble statues of Mephistopheles, Faust, Napoleon and Josephine. There is also a bronze statue of 'Mother and Child'.

Hartford invested heavily in Paradise Island. Not only did he build the Ocean Club, the Cloisters and the Versailles Gardens, but he also constructed an eighteen-hole golf course, created Hurricane Hole, developed riding stables, a restaurant and a water-taxi service from Nassau. His investments did not pay off and Hartford eventually sold all his holdings (including the Ocean Club) to the Mary Carter Paint Company, the American firm which later formed Resorts International Incorporated.

Resorts International

Resorts International has put Paradise Island firmly on the tourist map. In the late 1960s, its precursor, Mary Carter Paint, built the **Paradise Island Bridge** which links the island with New Providence. This toll bridge (paid for with tokens purchased for 50 cents) gave the access that was needed for tourists and locals alike. T.V. celebrity Merv Griffin bought Resorts International in the 1980s and brought further development to Paradise Island.

A small airport was constructed at the eastern end of Paradise Island in the 1980s. Merv Griffin's Paradise Island Airways fly between Paradise Island, Fort Lauderdale and Miami. Chalk's Airlines fly between Paradise Island and Bimini.

Night-life

Mary Carter Paint also built **Paradise Island Hotel**, now **Paradise Towers**, and a large casino which has recently been renovated. The casino sees action both day and night. There are slot machines, craps, roulette wheels and blackjack card tables. Adjoining the casino is **Le Cabaret Theatre** which produces performances nightly (except Sundays) in the Las Vegas style. The 'show of shows' has 'the glamour of Paris' and the 'excitement of Las Vegas' and includes local and American artists. Le Cabaret provides elaborate entertainment with a panoramic stage filled with a cast of over 50 artists. Costumes are colourful and the show is really spectacular. It has an ice-rink on stage: lions! tigers! Dazzling and magic.

Other night-life includes shows in the various hotels and visits to the numerous restaurants. In **Paradise Towers** (the new name of the Paradise Island Hotel) there are a variety of hostelries. **Café Martinique**, the oldest on Paradise Island, is renowned for French and continental cuisine. Try also the **Coyaba Room** in the **Britannia Towers** for Cantonese food, **Julie's** in the **Grand Hotel** for continental food, **Villa d'Este** for Italian cuisine and the **Bahamian Club** for continental and Bahamian dishes in the Paradise Towers Hotel. For seafood, try the **Blue Lagoon** and **Neptune's Table** (in the Holiday Inn). For a quiet and romantic evening, the **Courtyard Terrace** at the Ocean Club, which offers international cuisine, is a must.

Other attractions

Many visitors to Paradise Island will be content just visiting its beaches. On the northern side of the two vast hotels, **Britannia Towers** and the **Paradise Towers**, and the smaller more recently built **Grand Hotel** and the older **Ocean Club**, is a magnificent white sandy beach known for some reason as **Cabbage Beach**. It is a magnificent beach for walking, swimming, sunbathing and in rougher weather riding breakers. Watersports, including water-skiing and parasailing, are available.

Casuarina Drive takes you to another popular beach, **Paradise Beach**, known to tourists for nearly a century, which is near the north-western end of the island. Here you can wind-surf, water-ski, snorkel, and enjoy the paddle-boats.

Next to Paradise Beach is the **Holiday Inn**, the tallest hotel on Paradise Island. West of the Holiday Inn on Casuarina Drive is an area which formerly accommodated the **Porcupine Club**, an exclusive get-away for very wealthy Americans in the 1930s. **Club Méditerranée** (better know as Club Med), an international chain where tourists pay in advance and where beads instead of money are used to pay for extras, now occupies some of the land which was formerly used by the Porcupine Club.

A remote and private part of Paradise Island is at its western tip. It is the **Sivananda Yoga Retreat** established by Swami

Hurricane Hole, a safe haven for small craft (LISA ADDERLEY)

Vishundevananda who wrote *The Complete Illustrated Book of Yoga*. The retreat is spread out over four acres. Arrangements can be made to stay at the retreat and join in the special exercises, meditation and vegetarian meals.

Yachtsmen will want to dock at **Hurricane Hole**. Golfers will be attracted to the eighteen-hole **Paradise Island Golf Club** built by Huntingdon Hartford. On the northern side of the golf course is a quiet cove known as **Victoria Beach** where huge casuarinas grow near the water's edge.

At the other end of Paradise Island, on its western tip, is the first lighthouse to be constructed in The Bahamas. It still stands as a beacon marking the main entrance to Nassau harbour. You will have to go by boat to reach the lighthouse as there is no road on the western end of Paradise Island.

Paradise Island offers a great variety of activities both day and night for the adventurous visitor. Its restuarants, casino and the Le Cabaret show hold the glamour. Its quiet, beautiful beaches and clear aquamarine water hold the serenity that we all need on a vacation. So enjoy yourself!

| 5 |
Nassau – metropolis with a history

Introduction

Nassau is the political capital and the commercial hub of The Bahamas. Located on New Providence Island, it has grown from a quiet port to a bustling city with prettily laid out streets and inviting shops and arcades.

Nassau has a unique charm. Despite its now busy streets and rush-hour traffic jams, it exudes a beauty that is unmatchable. This is partly due to its preserved old world charm. Much of the ancient colonial architecture remains. A walk down the main street, the wide and well laid out Bay Street, originally called the Strand, will reveal signs of the Loyalist influence. Some of the patriots of the British cause emigrated to The Bahamas in the 1780s making it their home. They left their mark on The Bahamas and especially on its architecture, at least in the capital. While downtown Nassau, on the harbour-side, grew into a quaint and pretty little town housing the major businesses of The Bahamas which were owned by the white élite, less than a mile away, in Grant's Town or 'Over-the-Hill', little was done to plan the buildings or the layout. The black section of Nassau grew without supervision. It began as a swampy, wooded location and grew into a highly populated area, seething with life. Its houses were originally small clap-board edifices with porches and outside toilets. A few fruit trees grew in the small fenced-off yards. Small petty shops abounded.

The early town

Nassau was originally known as Charlestown. It was Nicholas Trott, the most successful Proprietory Governor, who laid out Charlestown anew in 1695 and renamed it Nassau in honour of the Prince of Orange-Nassau who became William III of England. In that year, the town comprised 160 houses, one church and two public houses. Trott built a fort which he named Nassau. The buildings were then mainly wooden with thatched roofs and were located around the

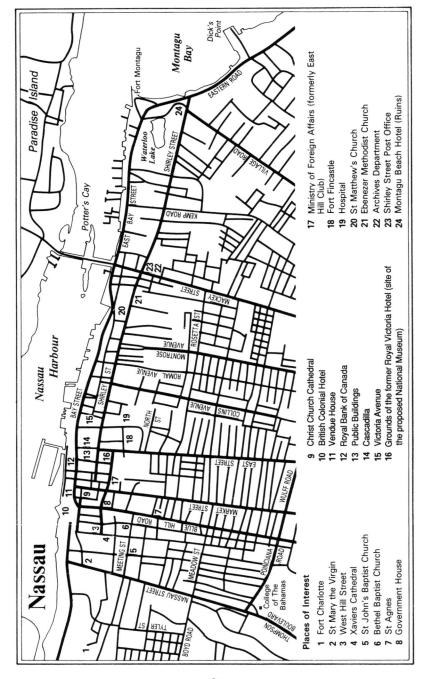

Nassau

Places of Interest

1 Fort Charlotte
2 St Mary the Virgin
3 West Hill Street
4 Xaviers Cathedral
5 St John's Baptist Church
6 Bethel Baptist Church
7 St Agnes
8 Government House

9 Christ Church Cathedral
10 British Colonial Hotel
11 Vendue House
12 Royal Bank of Canada
13 Public Buildings
14 Cascadilla
15 Victoria Avenue
16 Grounds of the former Royal Victoria Hotel (site of the proposed National Museum)

17 Ministry of Foreign Affairs (formerly East Hill Club)
18 Fort Fincastle
19 Hospital
20 St Matthew's Church
21 Ebenezer Methodist Church
22 Archives Department
23 Shirley Street Post Office
24 Montagu Beach Hotel (Ruins)

harbour that singled New Providence out as the most suitable seat of government.

However, from the late seventeenth century, Nassau was increasingly used by privateers and pirates as a base from which they attacked Spanish and French ships. Nassau was attacked and plundered several times. In October 1703 it was sacked by a combined Spanish and French fleet. Most of its inhabitants fled and those who stayed on New Providence 'lived scatteringly in little huts, ready upon any assault to secure themselves in the woods'.

Woodes Rogers and the town

Woodes Rogers' arrival made a difference. The first Royal Governor, Rogers arrived in 1718 to find the town in a dilapidated and dirty state. Fort Nassau was in shambles. Rogers immediately set every available man, including those pirates he had reformed, to work cleaning and rebuilding Nassau 'so that it began to have the appearance of a civilised place'. Fort Nassau was rebuilt, the town cleaned up, old houses were repaired and new ones built. During his second term as governor (1729-1732) Woodes Rogers called the first General Assembly. During its first session twelve Acts, including one to 'lay out the town of Nassau', were passed.

John Tinker and William Shirley

Further development of Nassau took place in the 1740s and 1750s during the Governorship of John Tinker (1738-1758) and William Shirley (1758-1768). Tinker was responsible for the restoration of Fort Nassau and the building of Fort Montagu under the guidance of the well-known military engineer, Peter Henry Bruce. By 1748 Bahamians, mainly from wealth gained through privateering, had further expanded the town. Tinker noted that New Providence had 'increased most surprisingly in strength and wealth, and the Town of Nassau [has] grown populous'.

Governor William Shirley initiated a new survey of the town, reclaiming much of the mosquito-infested swamp land so that the town could expand eastward. Among the many street which were laid out was Shirley Street, which still honours the Governor who created it. As yet, the streets were untarred.

The town in the early 1780s

By the early 1780s, Schoepf, a German traveller in The Bahamas

St Matthew's Church, Shirley Street (MICHAEL BOURNE)

who was touring the islands, described Nassau as a town hugging the 'hilly shore' with houses of wood, all lightly and simply built. The houses, few of which had glass windows, stood apart surrounded by trees, hedges and gardens. Schoepf described Nassau as having one fairly regular street or a line of houses which ran parallel to the water.

The Loyalist influence

Perhaps it was the Loyalists who had the most significant impact on Nassau's growth. Fleeing from the newly independent States of America, they brought a new energy and architectural style which they adapted to suit the needs of their new home in The Bahamas. They soon changed the appearance of Nassau 'into a town as well built as any . . . in the West Indies and one which promised to become distinguished for its beauty'. New streets were built, docks and wharves improved, a new jail and workhouse and a roofed market place were constructed. Thatched roofs were prohibited within the town of Nassau and all cemeteries had to be enclosed with walls and fences. Buildings constructed of large blocks of quarried stone, often with timber verandahs, louvred shutters, high-peaked roofs, dormer windows, brackets and lattice work, were also built. The buildings constructed by the Loyalists were well-designed and proportioned, nearly all of them being patterned after the English Georgian style with modifications to meet Bahamian climatic and economic conditions.

Nassau in the mid-nineteenth century

Nassau in 1844 was described as 'a sleepy town' of about 8,000 inhabitants with 'a population of idlers with maritime tastes'. The town, although still bounded on the west by West Street and the south by Hill Street (now East and West Hill), had some fine old Georgian colonial style residences. Four small boarding houses existed, the most prosperous being French's situated on West Hill Street. It is the present day Greycliff, a four-star restaurant and small hotel. Other houses which were built between the 1840s and 1860s included the East Hill Club which has recently been renovated and houses the Ministry of Foreign Affairs, Jacaranda on the south-west corner of Parliament Street and Cascadilla, on East Street.

Construction in the town accelerated in the mid-nineteenth

An old timbered house (MICHAEL BOURNE)

The water tower in Nassau (G. W. LENNOX)

century due mainly to the sudden flow of money brought in by the American Civil War (1861-1865). At the same time, Nassau was raised to the dignity of a city in 1861 and the tourist industry was boosted by the 1859 contract made between The Bahamas Government and Mr Samuel Cunard for a regular steamship connection between Nassau and New York. The Royal Victoria Hotel was built between 1859 and 1861. It soon became the headquarters of the daring blockade-runners. Nassau was used as an entrepôt for Confederate war materials. The Confederacy depended on exporting its cotton in order to survive and needed to obtain munitions to continue the war. The rebels thus had to evade President Lincoln's blockade of the southern part.

Nassau experienced a boom in its economy because of the increase in imports and exports. The new money led to more construction. Bay Street was widened and provided with lights for the first time. Sidewalks were curbed with granite from Union Street to Parliament Street. The north side of Bay Street was reclaimed and warehouses and shops were built. A new prison on East Street was built in 1865 and it was said that buildings sprung 'up like mushrooms after rain' while the value of land escalated by up to 400 per cent.

The town suffered from the slump which followed the ending of the American Civil War. However, Nassau benefited from the development of local industries, especially the sponge, pineapple and sisal industries in the late nineteenth century. Quite a number of new buildings, both public and private, were constructed between the 1870s and early 1900s. Further growth came with improvements in telecommunications after 1892 and the development of tourism in the twentieth century.

Modern times

Another period of rapid growth occurred in the 1920s and early 1930s. The passing of the Volstead Act in 1919 made Nassau and several other ports in The Bahamas centres for the trans-shipment of contraband liquor. English and Scottish liquor poured into Nassau and was sold by Nassau liquor merchants to 'bootleggers' who smuggled it into the United States. The profit to the Government from exports was phenomenal. A flurry of building followed. There were great improvements in public utilities, visitor accommodation and amenities. Warehouses were built along the waterfront to accommodate the volume of cases and barrels. An electricity plant, put into service in 1909, was enlarged and improved. A city water supply and sewerage system were installed and the Supreme Court building was constructed in 1921. To cope with the increased shipping, the harbour was dredged to a depth of twenty-five feet and Prince George Wharf was built. The mid-1920s witnessed a land boom in Nassau with large estates to the west of Nassau being developed. An air service between Nassau and Miami began in 1929, the year of the Wall Street crash. The Bahamas was to suffer slightly from the Depression and the end of Prohibition in 1933. However, the late 1930s saw an increase in winter tourists and the opening of new hotels and businesses. In 1940 the first airport, the Oakes Airfield, was officially inaugurated. This event marked the beginning of the modern era in Nassau's evolution. Since that time the growth in the tourist industry, banking and finance has been phenomenal. The money generated by those industries has transformed Nassau and New Providence. Nassau, once a 'quiet, sleepy hollow sort of place', is now a vibrant, hectic and bustling city. Its contrasting architectural styles show its colourful history and also demonstrate its modernity.

| 6 |
Walking tours of Nassau

Tour 1

Because of the traffic, it is better to explore the town of Nassau on foot. A good place to start is in **Rawson Square** in the centre of town. On the southern part of the square, which was recently renovated and landscaped, are the **Public Buildings**. Built between 1805 and 1813, the three buildings, which are based on Governor Tryon's Palace in New Bern, the ancient capital of North Carolina, originally housed the Post Office, the Legislative Council, Court Room (centre building), the Colonial Secretary's Office and Treasury (eastern building) and the House of Assembly, Surveyor-General's Office and Provost Marshal's Office (western building). When first constructed, the buildings overlooked the harbour – the sea came right up to Bay Street in front of the Public Buildings. In front of

A newly-painted surrey (MICHAEL BOURNE)

Walking Tours of Nassau

1   Water Tower
2   Fort Fincastle
3   Addington House
4   Police Headquarters

5   Zion Baptist Church
6   Former Royal Victoria Hotel and Garden
7   St Andrew's Presbyterian Church
8   Trinity Methodist Church

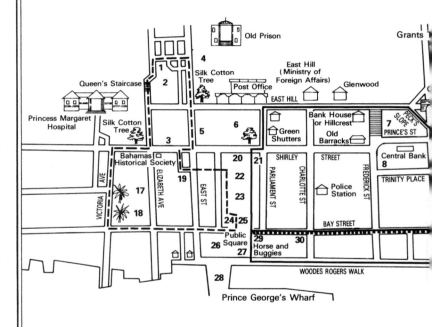

17   Victoria Court
18   Roval Palm
19   Cascadilla
20   Library
21   Cenotaph
22   Supreme Court
23   Queen Victoria's Statue
24   Public Buildings

25   House of Assembly
26   Churchill Building
27   Bust of Sir Milo Butler
28   Statue to Bahamian Women
29   Sunley Building
30   International Bazaar
31   Straw Market and Ministry of Tourism
32   Christ Church Cathedral

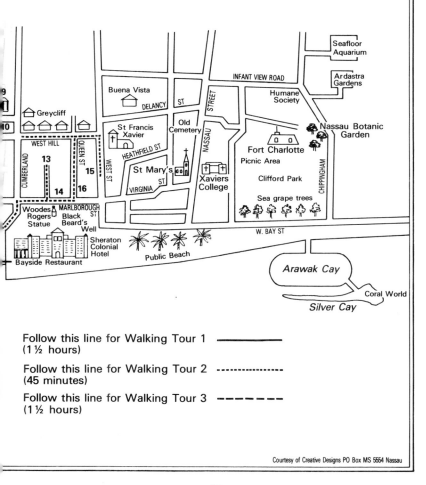

9	Government House	13	Ministry of Economic Affairs
10	Columbus Statue	14	Devonshire House
11	Parish Hall	15	Greek Orthodox Church
12	Princess House	16	US Embassy

Seafloor Aquarium

Ardastra Gardens

INFANT VIEW ROAD

Buena Vista

DELANCY ST

Greycliff

Humane Society

Nassau Botanic Garden

St Francis Xavier

Old Cemetery

Fort Charlotte

Picnic Area

HEATHFIELD ST

St Mary's

Clifford Park

WEST HILL

13

QUEEN ST

WEST ST

NASSAU STREET

STREET

CUMBERLAND

15

16

14

VIRGINIA ST

Xaviers College

Sea grape trees

CHIPPINGHAM

Woodes Rogers Statue

MARLBOROUGH ST

Black Beard's Well

W. BAY ST

Sheraton Colonial Hotel

Bayside Restaurant

Public Beach

Arawak Cay

Coral World

Silver Cay

Follow this line for Walking Tour 1 ——————
(1 ½ hours)

Follow this line for Walking Tour 2 ·················
(45 minutes)

Follow this line for Walking Tour 3 — — — — —
(1 ½ hours)

Courtesy of Creative Designs PO Box MS 5554 Nassau

the centre building is the statue of **Queen Victoria** which was given by the Imperial Order of the Daughters of the Empire in 1905. The western building now houses the **House of Assembly**, the centre the **Registry of the Supreme Court** and the **Publications Division** and the eastern a **Tourist Information Office.**

Across Bay Street on the northern part of the square is the bust of **Sir Milo Butler**, a national hero, and the first Bahamian to serve as Governor-General in an independent Bahamas. On the eastern side of the square is the **Churchill Building** which houses the Treasury and the Ministry of Finance. A walk northwards towards the harbour will take you to **Prince George Wharf** where cruise ships tie up. Luxury yachts and glass-bottomed boats which take visitors to the Sea Gardens moor there. There is also Randolph Johnston's statue of the Bahamian woman on Rawson Square.

Woodes Rogers' Walk runs parallel with the sea. In earlier days boats tied up at the landings along the walk. Today a few vendors of conch and fish are sometimes seen there. Backing on to Woodes Rogers' Walk is the **International Bazaar, Old Nassau**, the **Ministry of Tourism** and the **Straw Market**. The **Bayside Restaurant** at the rear of the **British Colonial Hotel** can also be seen as you stroll along the sea walk.

One of the oldest surviving buildings in the town (MICHAEL BOURNE)

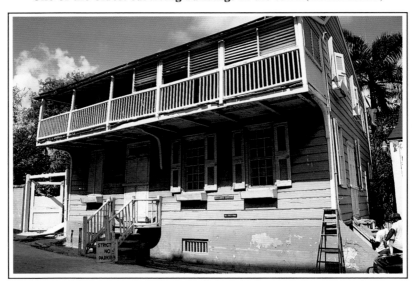

Returning to Bay Street and Rawson Square, turn right or west and stroll along the exciting main street. Very soon on the right you will pass the **Royal Bank of Canada** which first opened a branch in 1908. The present bank building was constructed in 1919. Nearby is the **International Bazaar** which lives up to its name. It has a variety of shops to tempt the most frugal spenders. There are other enticing shops before you arrive at the **Nassau Straw Market**, located on the site of the old **Public Market** which was razed by fire in 1974; the new market is located beneath the Ministry of Tourism's office buildings. There, Bahamian women (mainly) barter their straw-work, T-shirts, native jewellery, wood carvings and other knick-knacks. It is a lively place, seething with activity. The native straw-work, which includes baskets, dolls, hats and mats, is made by using the top of the thatch palm. The craft is an ancient one in The Bahamas. Much of the plait is woven in the Family Islands and long bands of it are rolled into a ball and sent into Nassau.

Continuing westward you will soon come to **Vendue House**, one of the oldest buildings in the city, which has been restored and converted into an Emancipation Museum, the **Pompey Museum**. It began as a single storey arcaded open building where merchants sold their goods at public auctions. It was there that slaves were sold. It faces on to **George Street**, one of the oldest streets in Nassau. Walk southward on George Street to **Christ Church Cathedral** on the left. Built in 1837, Christ Church stands on the site of a very early church. Its structure is of plain stone comprising a nave, a centre and two side aisles.

As you enter through the main door, notice the beautiful large stained-glass window over the altar. A new organ built by the Oberlinger Company of Germany has been installed. Just south of Christ Church is **Lex House**, thought to be one of the oldest houses in Nassau. It may have accommodated the Commander of the Spanish Garrison which occupied Nassau between 1782 and 1783. A local Attorney-at-Law purchased the property in 1978 and restored it beautifully. Continue up the hill passing **Georgeside** on the right. The house, which is kept in excellent condition by its owner, was built around 1860 and has an interesting collection of antique furniture. The two houses to the south of Georgeside are also quite old. On the corner is **Princess House** which has the jalousies, lattice and dormer windows which were characteristic of the Loyalist period. On the opposite side of the street is the Parish Hall of Christ

Christ Church Anglican Cathedral, Nassau (G. W. LENNOX)

Church Cathedral which dates back to the nineteenth century.
At the top of George Street is **Government House** which is built
on Mount Fitzwilliam. The front approach to the Governor's
residence is by steps. Midway up the steps is a statue of Christopher

Columbus, modelled in London by Washington Irving and imported by the Governor of that time, Sir James Carmichael Smyth, who gave it to the then Colony of the Bahamas.

If you continue along **Duke** and **Prince's Street** at the foot of the Government House steps, you will soon pass **Market Street** on the right. Look left or north and you will notice **Balcony House**, a late eighteenth century structure built of cedar probably by ships' carpenters. Its balcony is held up by wooden brackets and the internal staircase is said to be a ship's stairs. It has recently been restored by the Central Bank and converted into a 'Lifestyle Museum'. Notice **Gregory's Arch** which is an overpass to Government House. It was built during the governorship of John Gregory (1849-1854) and is named after him. Just to the east of it is **Peck's Slope**, named after Captain Peck, the Surveyor-General in 1874. Turning into Peck's Slope notice **St Andrew's Presbyterian Church**, the corner-stone of which was laid in 1810. Its portico, bell and tower were built in 1864. The Sunday School hall adjoins the church.

The top of Peck's Slope adjoins **East Hill Street**. There is a lovely view of Nassau and its harbour from the top of the hill. Turning east along East Hill Street, you will pass a property formerly called

Government House and the statue of Christopher Columbus
(LISA ADDERLEY)

Glenwood. A former Chief Justice, Thomas Walker, a friend of Governor Woodes Rogers, was buried here. It is believed that Woodes Rogers himself, who died in Nassau in July 1732, may also be buried in the grounds. Opposite is **Hillcrest** or St Andrew's Court, known also as Bank House. This quaint house, which is now occupied by a law firm, was once owned and occupied by Alfred E. Moseley, Editor of the morning paper, the *Nassau Guardian*, from 1887 to 1904. Bank House stands at the top of the Frederick Street steps.

Continue eastward to **East Hill** on the right. This ancient house, which has recently been renovated by the Williams family, now houses the Ministry of Foreign Affairs. The original house and old kitchen are believed to date back to the 1840s. The property, which has changed hands many times, was once owned by Lord Beaverbrook. It was, in more recent times, the East Hill Club which catered mainly to businessmen at lunch time.

Next to East Hill is the main **Post Office** where stamps are displayed. There are also periodic exhibitions of different sorts in the main foyer. The building also houses the Attorney General's office, the Registrar General's office, the Auditor General's office, the Ministry of Health and the Ministry of Transport.

From the main Post Office turn north on to **Parliament Street.** On the left is **Jacaranda**, a stately home built in the 1840s by the Chief Justice, Sir George Anderson, who included in its structure a load of ballast stones from Georgia purchased from a ship that came into Nassau Harbour. The house has a white-painted, low-pitched shingled roof, with wide latticed verandahs. The south side is covered with the traditional jalousies. Quoins, so typical of Bahamian architecture, can be seen at the corners of Jacaranda. Opposite Jacaranda are the grounds of the former Royal Victoria Hotel, built between 1859 and 1861 to accommodate the colourful blockade-runners. It was a very popular downtown hotel until it closed in the early 1970s.

Just south of Jacaranda is **Green Shutters**, a delightful pub and restaurant housed in a building which is over a hundred years old.

At the foot of **Parliament Street** cross **Shirley Street** and turn right. On the left is the **Nassau Public Library**, originally built as a prison between 1798 and 1800. Converted in 1873 it houses a fine

Nassau Public Library, originally built as a prison (MICHAEL BOURNE)

collection of Bahamiana including prints and some artefacts. If you continue either along Parliament Street or through the Garden of Remembrance, you will pass the **Cenotaph**, which has plaques commemorating those Bahamians who died in the First and Second World Wars. Wreaths are laid at this site once a year. Opposite the Cenotaph is the **Parliament Hotel**, a quaint three-storied structure believed to have been built in the 1930s.

Just north of the Cenotaph is the **Supreme Court Building**, which was constructed in 1921. North of the Supreme Court are the Public Buildings and Square where this tour began.

Tour 2

Another interesting walk starts at Rawson Square and ends at Greycliff on West Hill Street. Walk west along Bay Street past the Royal Bank of Canada, the Straw Market and Vendue House. Just to the west of Vendue House is the **British Colonial Hotel** which was designed in the Spanish American style, imported from South

The British Colonial Hotel (MICHAEL BOURNE)

Florida as the tourist industry began to emerge. It is built on the site of the old **Hotel Colonial** which was destroyed by fire in March 1922. The new hotel was opened in February 1923. In the front of the hotel is a statue of the first Royal Governor, Woodes Rogers. Also in the grounds of the hotel is a replica of **Blackbeard's Well**, named after the infamous pirate, Edward Teach.

Across the street from the hotel are two streets, **Nassau Court** and **Queen Street**; at the end of the former is the Ministry of Economic Affairs. The building formerly housed the Western Methodist Chapel, the Boys' Central School, the Government High School founded in 1925, the Ministry of Works and the Ministry of Tourism. Back on Marlborough Street, turn west towards Queen Street, which is still quaint and has an air of the past. **Number 16, Queen Street** is said to be two hundred years old and **Number 28**, with its ornate lattice work and traditional dormer windows, probably dates back to the mid-nineteenth century. **Devonshire House** or **Number 11, Queen Street** was built about 1840 and has outstanding features of early British Colonial architecture. It stands opposite the large modern office building which houses the **Embassy of The United States**. Many of the gardens are well kept and native foliage can be seen creeping over the walls that hug this interesting street. If you turn right at the top of the steps you will see the Roman Catholic Cathedral of **St Francis Xavier**, which was built between 1885 and 1887. Further down West Street is the Greek Orthodox Church, built in the 1930s to accommodate the small Greek community which, until the late 1930s, was mainly engaged in the sponge industry. Returning to West Hill Street and turning east you will pass **Postern Gate**, now a restaurant, **Ranora House** and **Sunningridge** situated at the top of Queen Street. There you will find the Sisters of Charity Convent which was founded in 1890. At the same time St Francis Xavier's Academy, a private school, was established. More recently it was moved to 'Westward Ho' near Fort Charlotte. On the south-east corner of West Hill Street and Balliou Hill Road is **Greycliff** which is partly hidden behind a high, hand-cut limestone block wall. It is now a four-star restaurant and also serves as a small hotel. It is a very old structure dating back to the late eighteenth century when it was believed to have housed the West Indian Garrison. It was later **French's Hotel**. This magnificent house has traditional lattice work, verandahs and a kitchen containing a fireplace which is set back from the main house.

Tour 3

Another walking tour starting at Rawson Square goes east along East Street to Fort Fincastle, down Elizabeth Avenue, east to Victoria Avenue and Bay Street and back to the Square.

Leaving Rawson Square, pass the Eastern Public Building, the Senate Building, the Supreme Court and the Nassau Public Library. Cross over **Bank Lane** passing the remains of an ancient house, of which only the old oven or fireplace remains, into East Street and then into **Miller's Court**. Go east on Miller's Court past an old house on the left, **Cascadilla**, now a real estate firm. Cascadilla dates back at least to the mid-nineteenth century. It was once occupied by Dr and Mrs William Kirkwood. Dr Kirkwood was a leading physician and a member of the Legislative Council. He practised medicine at Cascadilla. The house, which once stood on the eastern boundary of the town, was probably built by ships' carpenters as there are no mouldings or cornices. Part of the house, believed to be older

The late eighteenth-century house known as Greycliff, now a restaurant (GERALD SIMONS)

than the rest, is of very thick limestone. A small staircase leads to a third floor believed to have been a look-out. In the gardens there are ruins believed to have been slave dwellings. Cascadilla was also once owned by Edward George, son of John S. George, founder of John S. George Hardware Store. Sir Harold Christie also owned the house from 1953 until his death in the early 1970s.

Leaving Miller's Court, cross over Shirley Street on to **East Street**. At the corner of Shirley Street and East Street is the **Zion Baptist Church** which opened for public worship in 1835. A British Baptist Missionary, the Revd Joseph Burton, was its first pastor. Destroyed by the 1929 hurricane, the rebuilding of the church was undertaken by the Revd Talmadge Sands, the first Bahamian to head the church. He was ordained in March 1931. The present Minister, the Revd Charles Smith, has undertaken many additions and renovations in the church.

Walking south on East Street and crossing over East Hill Street, you will soon pass the **Police Headquarters** (once known as the Police Barracks) which was erected in 1900 on the site of the old Agricultural Gardens. The Barracks were built of much of the material of the old Military Barracks which were demolished at the end of the nineteenth century to make way for the Colonial Hotel.

Opposite the main entrance to the Police Headquarters is Prison Lane, a left turn off East Street. Follow Prison Lane up to the **Water Tower**. This imposing edifice was constructed on Bennet's Hill near to Fort Fincastle. Its purpose was to maintain water pressure throughout the city. It is 126 feet high and stands about 216 feet above sea-level. From the top of the tower there is a magnificent view of Nassau.

Next to the Water Tower is the much more ancient **Fort Fincastle**, built by Lord Dunmore in 1789. It is named for one of his titles. Seen from the north-east, it gives the appearance of an old paddle-wheel steamer. Originally it was mounted with two 24 pounders, two 32 pounders and two 12 pounders. Fort Fincastle served as a lighthouse until 1816 and subsequently as a signal tower.

To return to Nassau, leave Fort Fincastle and descend the **Queen's Staircase** or **66 Steps**. This steep staircase is believed to have been cut from solid limestone by slaves in the 1790s to provide an escape route from Fort Fincastle to the town. The steps were later named the **Queen's Staircase** in honour of Queen Victoria. A waterfall was built in more modern times to enhance the beauty of the steps.

The Queen's Staircase, said to have been cut by slaves in the 1790s (MICHAEL BOURNE)

The walk down Elizabeth Avenue to Shirley Street will take you past the **Princess Margaret Hospital** on the right. This was originally founded in 1809 and known as the Bahamas General Hospital. In 1955 it was renamed in honour of Princess Margaret's visit.

On the corner of Elizabeth Avenue and Shirley Street is the headquarters of the **Bahamas Historical Society**. Founded in 1959 to stimulate interest in Bahamian history, the Society boasts a museum and also sponsors monthly talks between January and June and September and December. The building originally belonged to the Queen Victoria Chapter of the Imperial Order of the Daughters of The Empire who gave it to the Society in 1976. The IODE planted out **Victoria Avenue** (which you should visit next) with Royal Palms in 1904. Some of the palms are still alive and greatly enhance the avenue, which was once a residential street. A few old houses still survive.

Leaving Victoria Avenue return on to Bay Street going west, passing **Moses' Plaza** which has a variety of business houses. Along Bay Street going towards Rawson Square there are a number of shops and plenty of browsing to be enjoyed on the way.

| 7 |

Grand Bahama – tourist resort and industrial centre

History

Grand Bahama is a very flat island which was once covered in pine trees. Its highest hill soars to a lofty 60 feet above sea-level. The most northerly island in the Bahama chain, it was ignored during early times because of its shallow waters and the treacherous Little Bahama Bank. In fact, wrecking was one of the chief occupations of its early inhabitants. After the erection of lighthouses in the 1850s and 1860s, wrecking was no longer a viable way of making a living.

The Lucayan Waterway which runs through the centre of the island of Grand Bahama (MICHAEL BOURNE)

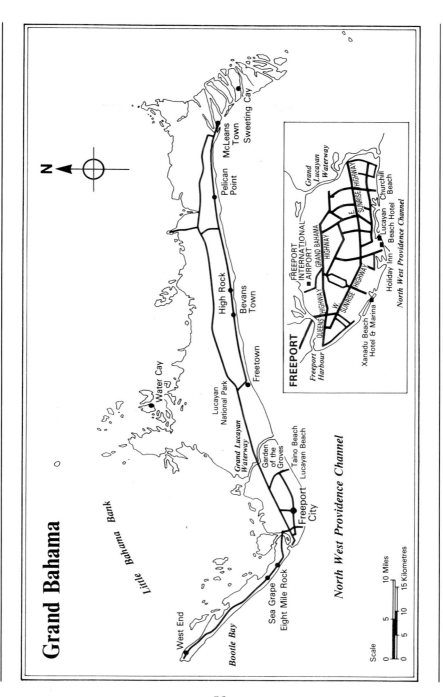

Grand Bahama

With the outbreak of the American Civil War in 1861, Grand Bahama, like Nassau and Bimini, was used as a depot for gun-running. In the 1920s and early 1930s, during Prohibition in the United States, Grand Bahama profited as an entrepôt for rum-runners.

Early settlement

It is believed that the original inhabitants of The Bahamas and Grand Bahama were the Siboney. This culture was superseded by the arrival of the Lucayans, a branch of the Arawak Indians who had their origin in South America. By 1520 the Lucayans had disappeared, having been transported to work in the gold and silver mines of Hispaniola and Cuba and in the pearl fisheries of Margarita, near Trinidad.

The Lucayans called the island Bahama and the Spanish who frequented the islands in the early years of their history named the island *Gran bajamar* (great shallows). Eventually the entire Bahamas are believed to have been named after these shallows.

It was inevitable that ships would be shipwrecked. A famous Spanish ship *Nuestra Senora de la Maravilla* was wrecked in the shallow waters not far from Memory Rock, which is north of West End. This ship has perhaps yielded the richest treasure of any wreck in The Bahamas.

First permanent settlement

After the demise of the Lucayans, the first permanent settlement, according to Peter Barratt, took place at **West End**. By 1836 its population numbered about 370; it had increased to 858 by 1861. Despite West End's involvement during the balmy years of the American Civil War, many inhabitants left to seek their fortunes in Nassau. West End was renowned for its involvement as a transhipment centre for liquor during Prohibition.

West End

West End is still a thriving town. Its main street abounds in shops, bars and houses. Something of its history can be seen in the **Star Hotel**, the first hotel built at the settlement on the island. At one point, as owner Austin Grant Jr recalls, it was patronised by only the rich and famous. Its fascinating bar is now open round the clock.

The settlement of West End was best known for the **Grand Bahama Hotel** once operated by the Jack Tar chain. It was a well-equipped hotel standing on the site of the ill-fated Butlins 'holiday camp' which opened in February 1950 and closed ten months later. The hotel boasted an eighteen-hole golf course, a swimming pool, restaurants, bars and a night-club. This end of Grand Bahama is the nearest part of the island to the United States, being only about 55 miles away.

Eight Mile Rock
After Prohibition, the Commissioner (the chief administrator for the district) was moved from West End to **Eight Mile Rock**, named for its eight miles of rocky shore which runs east to west along **Hawksbill Creek**. A suburb of Freeport, Eight Mile Rock is the headquarters of the Commissioner. Across Hawksbill Creek are several towns including **Pinder's Point, Lewis Yard** and **Hunter's**. Pinder's Point is known for its two fine restaurants which serve excellent food and also provide a good atmosphere.

Along the coastline of Eight Mile Rock is an interesting **'boiling hole'**. Pinder's Point also has a boiling hole, known as the **Chimney**, under which is a cave system.

On the way to Freeport
Approaching Freeport from the south are **William's Town** and **Russell Town** which are located on a breathtaking stretch of beach. They were named for local patriarchs of the area. Other communities which hug the shore are **Smith's Point** and **Mather Town**. Strictly speaking they are in Freeport but lie outside the bounded area.

Freeport – The Bahamas' second city
Just over three decades ago, the city that is now Freeport was nothing more than a pine forest. The establishment and growth of Freeport has been phenomenal. It was the brainchild of an American financier, the late Wallace Groves, who saw the possibility for the area's development. Groves came to The Bahamas in the mid-1940s when he bought a lumber company at Pineridge. He also owned Little Whale Cay, which served as a retreat for him.

Groves proposed that a free port and industrial tourist area should be developed on Grand Bahama. In 1955, after some negotiation with The Bahamas Government, Groves and his company, the Grand Bahama Port Authority Ltd, were granted 50,000 acres of land with an option of a further 50,000. The Port Authority agreed in turn

that it would build a free port and industrial centre. By the Hawksbill Creek Agreement in 1955, concessions were granted guaranteeing freedom from taxation of income, capital gains, real estate or personal property until 1985 (later extended to 1990) and from all customs and excise duties (except on goods for personal use) until 2054 and also freedom from immigration restrictions (nullified by an Act of 1970). Freeport developed slowly. Groves encouraged the shipping tycoon D.K. Ludwig to develop a large harbour. A ship-bunkering terminal was the first major industry. In one month, soon after its establishment, it exported almost one million barrels of oil duty free. Another industry, a cement producing plant, was established in 1961.

A year earlier Groves had signed the Supplement Agreement with the Government. The agreement required the port to build a 200-room hotel and allowed it to purchase more land. Groves and Louis Chesler, a Canadian businessman, formed the Grand Bahama Development Company and began the development of Lucaya. They built the luxurious Lucayan Beach Hotel which was opened in late 1963. The hotel had a large gambling casino, something unique at the time.

Industrial development continued. A $100-million oil refinery was built. By 1970, however, recession in the United States had begun to affect The Bahamas and at the same time the Government's Bahamianisation policy challenged the licences of the Port Authority. At this time, after the Prime Minister's famous 'bend or break' speech, a number of foreigners left Grand Bahama. By the end of the decade, however, Freeport was again a thriving commercial and industrial area.

Freeport is today the second most important tourist centre in The Bahamas. It is equipped with first-class hotels, excellent entertainment and superb restaurants and sporting facilities.

Places to see in Freeport

If you arrive by air, you are bound to pass Independence Circle on your way into town. Travelling along the **Mall** you will pass several Government offices, including the main Post Office and the Royal Bank of Canada.

At the intersection of the Mall and Pioneer's Way is the head-

Putting the finishing touches to a straw basket (MICHAEL BOURNE)

quarters of the Grand Bahama Port Authority. Continuing along the Mall you will come to **Ranfurly Circus**, named for a British Governor, the Earl of Ranfurly (1953-57). At this intersection is located the world-famous **International Bazaar**, the **Princess Tower Hotel and Casino** and the **Princess Country Club**.

This complex is perhaps the most exciting area in Freeport. The International Bazaar, designed and decorated in the style of many different countries, has a large number of shops which offer English china, crystal, photographic equipment, jewellery, perfume, clothing and much more. There are many restaurants and cafes. Wandering through the Bazaar with its quaint, narrow streets you feel the atmosphere of Paris and Montmartre, North Africa and Hong Kong, China, Spain and Mexico.

There is also a **Bahamian Straw Market** on the **Churchill Pub** side of the Bazaar. All types of straw work can be purchased here.

Night-life is also a feature of the area. You can gamble day and night at the **Princess Casino** with its Moorish-style building next door to the Bazaar. There is also an extravagant show which will lure some.

Palm trees in the garden of the Princess Casino, Freeport
(G. W. LENNOX)

One of the largest resorts of its kind, The Bahamas Princess Resort and Casino has about 1,000 rooms and includes the **Princess Casino**, the **Princess Towers** and the **Princess Country Club**.

The **Princess Towers Hotel**, with its beautifully tiled reception area, offers very comfortable accommodation and excellent sporting facilities including a large swimming pool, numerous tennis courts, a golf course, a bus service to and from the beach and a marina.

Across the road from the Towers is the Princess Country Club which is built around a plaza and swimming pool with its own waterfall. The **John B** restaurant, which is a must, is adjacent.

West of Ranfurly Circle is **Bahamia**, a sought-after residential area. Continuing along the South Mall, you will soon come to the **Xanadu Beach Hotel**, once the private domain of the late billionaire recluse Howard Hughes. The Xanadu Beach Hotel has its own marina. Gas and diesel fuel are available. The hotel also has excellent tennis facilities, a pool, and a fine beach.

If you travel east from the Ranfurly Circle you pass the **Pub on the Mall** (Freeport is known for its English pubs), a **Shrine** at Mary Star of the Sea Church and the Sunrise Shopping Centre.

Lucaya

Continuing eastwards, you soon come to Lucaya Circle and the area of Lucaya. To the south is a lovely white sand beach bounded by some fine hotels. These include the newly refurbished **Lucayan Beach Hotel and Casino**, the original hotel in the area. Nearby is the **Atlantic Beach Hotel** and the **Holiday Inn**. The man-made **Lucayan Marina** is to the north of the waterfront hotels. It contains the largest yacht basin on the island.

For the visitor who enjoys the sun and sport this area is paradise. Here, you can embark on fishing trips, snorkelling, and for the more intrepid, scuba-diving sponsored by the Underwater Explorers Society (UNEXSO). There is also an opportunity to try parasailing and wind-surfing. At night, enjoy the many restaurants, bars and shows offered in the **Panache Night Club**, the **Holiday Inn** and **Studio 69**.

Exploring further afield

While in Freeport it is worth visiting the outlying settlements. You should also visit several other places of interest such as **Old Free Town**, known for its blue holes, **Gold Rock**, which has the highest sand dunes on the island, and **High Rock**, the administrative centre for eastern Grand Bahama, which is located on a low bluff. It boasts good restaurants and has a police station and a public library. Further east along the coast is **Pelican Point**, which has perhaps the widest beach on the island. **Rock Creek** is a tiny village with a 'blue hole' which teems with marine life. Still further east is **McLean Town** known for its **Conch-cracking contest** held once a year on Columbus Day. The object of the contest is to see who can break and clean the most conchs in a given time.

Going further east must be done by boat. Across Rumer's Cay is **Deep Water Cay** which has a few small guest-houses and a small airstrip. The most easterly settlement is **Sweeting's Cay** first settled by spongers and now a place where tourists and yachtsmen can refresh themselves.

Peter Barratt, the local Grand Bahamian historian, advises that the best way to travel is by private taxi or rented car. He recommends stopping at the **Rand Nature Centre** which is in close proximity to Freeport. It offers alluring nature trails through a nature reserve.

Another must is the **Garden of The Groves** and the **Grand Bahama Museum**. The splendidly designed botanical Garden of The Groves contains trees, shrubs and flowers from all over the world. There are waterfalls, a fern gully and the national bird of The Bahamas, the fantastic flamingo.

The Museum records the history of the island in many attractive and unique visual and audio-visual displays. It is particularly strong on the early Lucayan culture, marine life and the piracy period. It also captures the early development of Hawksbill Creek and the social life of the earlier era.

About 13 miles from the Garden of the Groves is the **Lucayan National Park**, a lovely pine forest. The route to the park will take you over the magnificent **Grand Lucayan Waterway**, a canal that bisects the island of Grand Bahama. The park contains the 'largest explored underwater cave system in the world'.

Freeport has in its short history developed a character of its own. It is very different to the ancient capital, Nassau. As Barratt has described, it does not encourage a 'street society' and people rarely walk anywhere. Some Bahamians criticise the second city for its absence of 'soul'. When they visit Freeport, however, they marvel

The Garden of the Groves (G. W. LENNOX)

and enjoy the wide, clean streets and the efficient water, electrical and telephone services. Freeport is indeed a modern, growing city with a resilient and optimistic population – one that has faith in its future development.

| 8 |
The Family Islands

Introduction

Out from Nassau, the Family Islands are scattered over the blue-green waters of the Atlantic. Not all of the 700 islands and cays are inhabited. Some are large with goodly-sized populations, others are small and uninhabited. Each island has its own character, but is still distinctly Bahamian. It is in the Family Islands that you can experience peace and serenity, witness breathtaking ocean and beach views, enjoy watersports, fishing and quiet picnics and yet experience pulsating music and dancing at night.

Accommodation varies in the Family Islands. There are luxurious first-class hotels and more modest but comfortable guest-houses. Wherever you stay, the people exude a warmth and friendliness that will keep you coming back.

There is a wide variety of foods. Fish, especially the succulent grouper, is a speciality. Lobster (known as crawfish in The Bahamas) is another. Conch (pronounced 'konk') is a Bahamian favourite and is prepared in many different ways – chowder, salad, fritters are just a few.

Travel to the islands is usually by Bahamasair, the national flag-carrier, from Nassau, the capital of The Bahamas. If you prefer to be more leisurely and adventurous you can go by Bahamian mail-boat. Some airlines, with small aircrafts, can bring you from ports in Florida such as Miami, Fort Lauderdale and Palm Beach into the Abacos and North Eleuthera.

Abaco – a yachtsman's paradise

Introduction

Abaco and its cays are cherished by yachtsmen. The beautiful aquamarine waters are almost indescribable. The atmosphere of the

The Family Island Regatta, George Town, which takes place each April (overleaf) (BAHAMAS NEWS BUREAU)

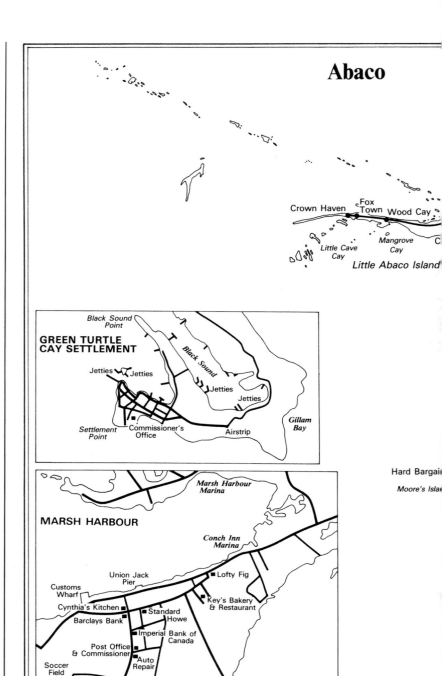

Abaco

Crown Haven
Fox Town
Wood Cay

Little Cave Cay

Mangrove Cay

Little Abaco Island

GREEN TURTLE CAY SETTLEMENT

Black Sound Point

Black Sound

Jetties

Jetties

Jetties

Jetties

Settlement Point

Commissioner's Office

Airstrip

Gillam Bay

Hard Bargain

Moore's Island

MARSH HARBOUR

Marsh Harbour Marina

Conch Inn Marina

Union Jack Pier

Lofty Fig

Customs Wharf

Cynthia's Kitchen

Key's Bakery & Restaurant

Standard Howe

Barclays Bank

Imperial Bank of Canada

Post Office & Commissioner

Auto Repair

Soccer Field

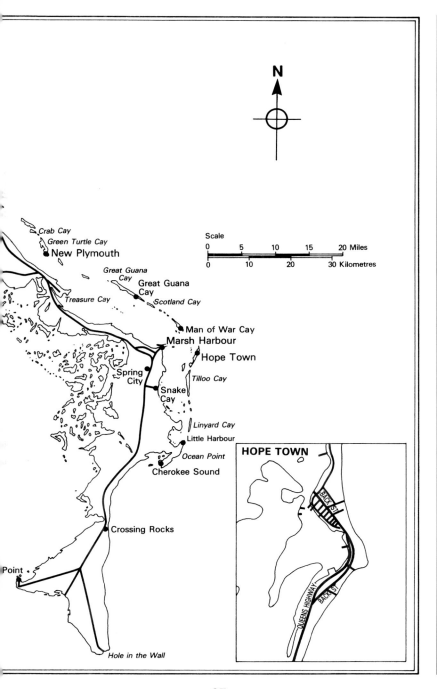

Crab Cay
Green Turtle Cay
New Plymouth

Great Guana
Cay
Great Guana
Cay
Treasure Cay
Scotland Cay

Man of War Cay
Marsh Harbour
Hope Town

Spring
City
Tilloo Cay
Snake
Cay

Linyard Cay
Little Harbour
Ocean Point
Cherokee Sound

Crossing Rocks

Point

Hole in the Wall

Scale
0   5   10   15   20 Miles
0   10   20   30 Kilometres

N

HOPE TOWN
BACK ST.
QUEENS HIGHWAY
BACK ST.

cays bears a resemblance to New England from which it attracts so many of its visitors and winter residents. Abaco has many cays spread over an area of over 130 square miles of water. Its two major islands, Great and Little Abaco, have a myriad of small cays flanking the mainland. The sea channel between the islands allows for good cruising.

Abaco is in the northern Bahamas and typically boasts pine forests. It still has enough woodland for hunters to come to shoot wild boar and ducks. Its waters abound with fish, including the marlin and sailfish. It also has bonefishing flats.

For the landlubbers, the best way to get to Abaco is by Bahamasair from Nassau to Treasure Cay or Marsh Harbour. There are also flights from Fort Lauderdale, Palm Beach and other parts of Florida.

Northern cays

There are dozens of cays of different sizes. Many are quite small and uninhabited. Some are one-resort islands and others have prettily laid out villages dating back to Loyalist times.

Yachtsmen might wish to start their exploration of the Abacos at **Walker's Cay** which is the northernmost island in the Abacos. It has the **Walker's Cay Hotel and Marina** which has space for 75 boats. It also has petroleum products and services and a small airstrip. A little to the south are the **Grand Cays** which have an anchorage. A small number of people live at the main settlement which boasts several restaurants and a small hotel. There are many other small cays which are worth a visit. Sailing enthusiasts should consult the latest *Yachtsman's Guide to The Bahamas* for excellent information on the cays.

Little Abaco

For those who must stay on land, **Crown Haven** and **Fox Town** on Little Abaco are the places to go. The latter is a picturesque settlement with a small seven-room hotel and a restaurant which specialises in Bahamian foods.

Great Abaco

On the way to **Cooper's Town** pass through **Cedar Harbour**, another small settlement. Cooper's Town is the main and largest settlement on the north end of Great Abaco. It is the headquarters for the Commissioner. The settlement has a hardware store, grocery shops, liquor outlets, a telephone station and a small laundromat. Recommended restaurants are **M and M and Bar**, and **Sammie's Restaurant and Bar**.

Green Turtle Cay

After passing the two small villages of **Grape Tree** and **Blackwood** you come to the ferry which runs over to **New Plymouth, Green Turtle Cay** several times a day, usually after a scheduled airliner has landed. The two-mile trip on Floyd Lowe's water taxi takes only about 15 minutes to the settlement of **New Plymouth**, a well-preserved, picturesque and prosperous settlement. Its economy, based mainly on crawfishing, is a buoyant one. Established by Loyalists, who also brought slaves with them, New Plymouth still retains a unique old world charm. Its pastel coloured clapboard houses, which have varying degrees of fretwork, indicate its history and the character of its people.

Particularly attractive is the **Albert Lowe Museum**, named after a local maker of model ships, the late father of the world renowned artist Alton Lowe who established it. The Museum contains displays of model ships, various historical artefacts, original Alton Lowe

**The Loyalist Sculpture Garden, Green Turtle Cay,
Abaco** (GAIL SAUNDERS)

paintings and photographs of what life was like in olden times. Its curator, Mrs Ivy Roberts, who lives next door, takes delight in showing visitors around.

Not too far from the museum is the **Memorial Sculpture Garden** opposite the **New Plymouth Inn**. The Sculpture Garden contains busts of some 30 Bahamians who represent different islands of The Bahamas. Many of those represented have Loyalist roots.

The New Plymouth Inn, which has been restored with the traditional 'gingerbread house' decorations, has comfortable and modest accommodation; it also has a restaurant. There are several smaller guest-houses in New Plymouth and several restaurants including **McIntosh's Sea View Restaurant and Bar**, and Vena Bethel's **Plymouth Rock**, next to the town pier. There is also Miss Emilie's happy **Blue Bee Bar**. There are a number of gift shops including **Loyalist Shop, Shell Hut, Loyalist Rose** and **Randy's Gift Shop**.

Nearby at White Sound is the **Green Turtle Cay Club** which also has a yacht club. Both of these are reached by boat. A fine restaurant overlooking the harbour is run by the proprietors of the Green Turtle Cay Club. The Green Turtle Cay Yacht Club is known for its June Invitational Fishing Tournament and its Regatta Week in early July.

Another resort not far from New Plymouth is the **Bluff House Club** situated on a 100-foot hill with a commanding view of the water. It also offers a fine restaurant and excellent marine facilities.

Treasure Cay

Back on the mainland not far from the ferry (by car or bus) is **Treasure Cay**, a luxury resort development. It lies on the mainland and is not really a cay. It has a beautiful three-mile beach. The development, which dates back to the late 1950s, features the **Treasure Cay Beach Hotel** which is equipped with a modern marina, numerous swimming pools, tennis courts, an eighteen-hole golf course, a restaurant, a shopping complex, post office, sail-boat rentals, water-skiing and a dive shop which sponsors daily snorkel and scuba trips and fishing charters. In the shopping complex there are a variety of retail outlets including a pharmacy, a straw work shop, gift shops, a telephone service, beauty salon and bicycle rental.

Besides catering to short term tourists, Treasure Cay also has many private homes, villas and condominiums which have time-sharing facilities. There is also a real estate office at Treasure Cay.

Treasure Cay Beach (GAIL SAUNDERS)

Carleton Point

At the northern end of the Treasure Cay property is **Carleton Point**, which was Abaco's first settlement. In 1783, about 600 Loyalist refugees from New York, fleeing the newly independent United States, settled at Abaco and 'laid out a town . . . called Carleton'. Carleton was named after Sir Guy Carleton, a British military commander of North America stationed in New York. These first settlers of Abaco optimistically hoped to develop a major commercial and agricultural centre. Unfortunately, due to civil strife, harsh agricultural conditions and a devastating hurricane, the settlers began to leave, soon abandoning the town altogether. For years no one knew the location of the settlement. It was not until 1979 that Professor Steve Dodge was able, with the help of the Department of Lands and Surveys and the Department of Archives, to locate the eighteenth century site. Since that time, some archaeological work has been carried out by Mr Bob Carr, archaeologist for the Historic

Preservation Division, Dade County, Florida. Several artefacts from the site are now in the custody of the Albert Lowe Museum. They remain the property of the Government of The Bahamas.

In 1983, a bronze historical plaque was placed at Carleton Point near the original settlement. The plaque and ceremony commemorated the bicentennial of the founding of the town in September, 1783. The energetic explorer may wish to approach it from the Treasure Cay Beach. It is a two-mile walk from the Treasure Cay Hotel. Comfortable shoes are needed for the last part of the journey which is a bit rough.

March Harbour

The commercial centre of Great Abaco is Marsh Harbour. It is about three-quarters of an hour car ride from Treasure Cay. It is also accessible by boat. Its harbour is easy to enter and is sheltered from strong westerly winds.

Marsh Harbour has a variety of modern food stores, department and hardware stores. There are also branches of some of the leading banks, many restaurants, a beauty salon, gas stations and time-sharing facitilies. Convenient places to stay are the **Conch Inn and Marina** which suits both yachtsmen and landlubbers. Its marina accommodates 65 yachts and all fuel and yachting facilities are available. The hotel offers spacious rooms, a bar and restaurant, a pool, an attractive boutique and a magnificent view of the harbour.

Other marinas include **Triple J** and **Marsh Harbour Marine**. Bareboat Yacht charters can be obtained from **Bahamas Yachting Services**.

A newer resort complex which is very near to the Conch Inn is **Abaco Towns by the Sea** which offers time-sharing facilities.

Nearby (you can take a short cut through the woods) is the **Great Abaco Beach Hotel and Marina**. First opened in 1979 by Abaco businessman Leonard Thompson, it has recently changed ownership. Peter Sweeting, a Nassau businessman, now heads the new company, Boat Harbour Marina and Resorts, that owns the hotel. The latter has 20 rooms and five two-bedroom villas. The rooms in the hotel are spacious and overlook the well-manicured grounds, the beach and swimming pool. There are also a pool and tennis courts. The hotel has an atmosphere-filled restaurant and bar.

The Great Abaco Hotel is within walking distance of the ferry, which was founded by Marcel Albury and is still run by the Albury family. The ferry provides the main transportation between the mainland and the cays. It is a treat to visit the various cays for an afternoon or for a longer time.

Hope Town

Hope Town is a short ferry ride from Marsh Harbour. Located on Elbow Cay, its entrance is marked by the red and white candy-striped lighthouse, perhaps the most photographed lighthouse in The Bahamas. It guards an excellent harbour, around most of which is located the picturesque village of Hope Town.

The main street in Hope Town (GAIL SAUNDERS)

Brief history

After the American Revolutionary War, thousands of Loyalists settled in The Bahamas. A widow from Charleston, South Carolina, by the name of Wyannie Malone, along with her four children, settled at Hope Town in about 1785. Her children and grand-children, who inter-married or married the children of migrants from Harbour Island, helped to establish and develop the town. The names Malone, Russell, Bethel, Carey, Lowe, Sawyer and Thompson still survive. Hope Town remained mostly poor, with its inhabitants living at a subsistence level based on fishing and farming. Hope Towners also benefited from ships which were wrecked on Elbow Reef, which is located to the east and north-east of the settlement. Even clergymen saw no harm in getting the congregation on their knees to pray so that they got to the reef first. When the lighthouse was completed in 1863 the wrecking business declined.

Hope Towners have also been involved in the pineapple and sisal industries, which both peaked in the late nineteenth century and declined in the early twentieth. Sponging, which sustained The Bahamas' ecomony for nearly three-quarters of a century, also brought profits for the population of Hope Town and the Abacos. Similarly many Abaconians and Hope Towners worked at Wilson City, a lumber town established in 1906 on the mainland. The Bahamas Timber Company, which built a sawmill, a railway and provided houses for its labourers, had modern amenities such as electricity and an ice plant. Besides supplying jobs, Wilson City also provided a market for fish and agricultural produce. Its closure in 1916 was a blow to many Hope Town people.

Abaco and Hope Town are also known for their ship-building tradition. One of the largest ships ever built in Abaco, and the second largest to be built in The Bahamas, the *Abaco Bahamas*, was built by Jenkens Roberts of Hope Town in 1917. Ships were necessary for travel between all the many cays and islands and to carry freight of varying sorts – sponge, pineapple, sisal and lumber.

It was in the post-Second World War days that Hope Town, an isolated settlement, began to be exposed and discovered. Visitors from the United States, especially yachtsmen, began to frequent Hope Town. Some built winter retreats. Burl Ives, for example, built a house some miles south of the settlement.

Gradually tourism developed. At first it was on a small scale, but many tourists built houses and also hired local people as fishermen and employed them as caretakers for their houses. Today, Hope Town is a thriving settlement catering to yachtsmen, winter residents, and to tourists. It has a few first-class hotels, fine restaurants, grocery shops (visit especially **Vernon's Grocery**), marine stores, drug stores, boat rentals and gift shops – especially important is the **Ebb Tide Gift Shop**. For real estate, visit **Malone Estates**. For some of the finest Bahamian or American food, visit **Rudy's Place** which is just ouside Hope Town. In fact, this restaurant and the two others, the **Elbow Cay Beach Inn** and the **Abaco Inn** located at **White Sound** on the eastern side of Elbow Cay, provide free transportation.

Where to stay and what to see

For a short stay, the most convenient place to stay is the **Hope Town Harbour Lodge** which has 21 clean and comfortable rooms. It faces the main harbour and also overlooks the Atlantic Ocean. The food is delicious at the Lodge; a pool, a beach and a few cottages are also available.

The Elbow Cay Beach Inn is south-west of the town and the Abaco Inn, located in White Sound, is just 1 ½ miles south of Hope Town. It has a restaurant, bar, cottages and a swimming pool and overlooks the waters of White Sound. On the west side there is calm water with a sandy beach; on the east side it is rougher.

There is much to see in this little town. First equip yourself with *A Guide and History of Hope Town* by Steve Dodge and Vernon Malone (a Hope Towner). If time permits, read this information-packed booklet which tells you about the history and most interesting places to visit in Hope Town. If you have only a brief time, do not miss the **Wyannie Malone Historical Museum** which is located in an historic house. The Museum, which contains many artefacts including photographs, maps, furniture, household utensils and the like, was founded by a group of interested Hope Towners who wished to preserve Hope Town's culture and history. The project, spearheaded by the late Byrle Malone Patterson, has grown and the Museum is staffed by volunteers. Members who pay dues annually support the upkeep of the Museum along with entrance fees. There is a Hope Town Heritage Day held each year.

Near to the **Public Dock** is the **Post Office, Police Station, Commissioner's Office** and **Jail**. Along **Back Street** to the north is the **Ebb Tide Gift Shop** and **St James Methodist Church** which

The Wyannie Malone Historical Museum, Hope Town
(GAIL SAUNDERS)

has been rebuilt after having been destroyed by fire. Walk along Back Street past the **Hope Town Fire house,** the **Cholera Graveyard,** the **Native Touches Gift Shop, Edith's Straw Market** (which sells native straw goods) and the **Ball Park.** Nearby on Freeport Lane, almost on Bay Street, is **Winer Malone's Shed** where Mr Malone, the famed boat-builder, constructs the Abaco dinghies using only hand tools and natural crook timber for frames.

There is also the oldest house in Hope Town, now the home of the Museum, on Back Street near to **Hope Town Harbour Lodge.** Not far from it is **Batelco's Office** and the **Hope Town School.** The beach on the eastern side of the island is inviting.

The **Lighthouse** can be visited during the day. Ask a dinghy owner at the Public Dock. A guide will show you around and will tell you how the lighthouse works.

There are several marinas in Hope Town including the

Lighthouse Marina, the **Hope Town Marina** and the **Sea Horse Marina**. There is also **Abaco Bahamas Charters** which has a large number of boats to rent.

Hope Town is a quiet, peaceful but busy settlement. It offers a variety of activities and will be enjoyed by anyone who takes the time to visit it. Hope Town people are so friendly that you will want to return again and again.

Man-O-War Cay

Close to Hope Town and a short ferry ride from Marsh Harbour is Man-O-War Cay, world renowned for boat-building. Its sheltered harbour must be approached with caution. The westerly channel leads to the Man-O-War Marina which accommodates boats drawing up to six feet.

Man-O-War is a small (only two and a half miles long and less than half a mile wide), peaceful, well-kept town. Its clean, narrow streets, which are mostly paved with cement, are used by pedestrians, motorbikes and golf carts. The houses are mostly wooden, and are painted in a variety of pastel colours. Flowers, seagrape trees and other colourful shrubs abound throughout the well-kept settlement.

Boat-building is the biggest industry on Man-O-War Cay and perhaps the oldest. It is believed that the Loyalists greatly influenced the craft of boat-building which has been passed down from generation to generation.

Boats are built at several locations or yards at Man-O-War Cay. Most boats built here are fibreglass boats although some are still built of lumber. The oldest boatyard, established in 1888, is owned by William Albury. Other well-known boat-builders are Willard and Benny Albury. They specialise in the popular Man-O-War boats. Edwin Albury, who runs the two largest operations at the cay, and Joe Albury, who builds sailing dinghies, half-size models and wooden furniture, are also well-known boat-builders. The Albury family run everything. The story goes that if you should ask for Mr and Mrs Albury on Man-O-War, the whole island will stand up!

There are a variety of things for the visitor to do. Lunch and dinner, either sit down or take-away, can be had at **Dock'n'Dine** located at the head of the main dock. For take-away only, try **Bite Site**. There is a park across the street from the snack bar where you can eat at benches and tables.

For shopping try **Sandy Albury's** gift shop, the **Seaside Shop** which sells Bahamian hand prints and Androsia batik, and the **Sail Shop**. The latter, run by Misses Lina, Lois, Mary and Patricia, makes world-renowned duffle bags, tote bags, yachting jackets, hats and other accessories. It no longer repairs sails, however. There are also several bakeries and other stores that sell groceries and fruit. There is a Post Office and a telephone station where you will meet Haziel Albury, former schoolteacher and author of *Man-O-War, My Island Home*, a personal history of the cay. Mr Albury and his wife Mary of the Sail Shop will tell you all you need to know and more about Man-O-War.

Great Guana Cay

To the north of Man-O-War is Great Guana Cay. Albury's ferry runs there twice a week or by special charter. The cay, which has only about 100 people, has some of the loveliest beaches in Abaco. There is one small hotel, the Guana Beach Resort, which has a dock. The hotel serves delicious food. In addition there are a few grocery shops and Milo Pinder's gift shop which sells T-shirts, some shell jewellery and an assortment of souvenirs.

The settlement itself is small but pretty. There are many coconut palms and casuarinas which line the white sandy, but almost deserted, beaches. At its northern tip is a new development called **Treasure Island**, where cruise ships come in bi-weekly.

Little Harbour

Little Harbour is well worth a visit. Take a boat from Marsh Harbour to this small settlement, the home of sculptor Randolph Johnston and his talented family. The Johnstons maintain a foundry, a shop and a studio. Randolph Johnston is known for such Bahamian bronze sculptures as the **Monument to Bahamian Women, Sir Milo Butler** and others. The former bronze can be seen in Rawson Square. He has also done other large sculptures of dolphins and creatures of the sea which are now in the States.

Randolph's son, Pete, has a pub near the harbour. It is occasionally open in the evenings.

The Little Harbour cliff is protected under The Bahamas National Trust. This means that no spear-fishing or removal of flora, fauna or turtle eggs is allowed. Explore the small cays nearby by dinghy and let nature and its beauty do the entertaining.

Cherokee Sound and Cherokee

South of Little Harbour is Cherokee Sound which has an anchorage fairly near to the settlement of Cherokee. This small settlement can also be approached now by motor vehicle. Cherokee is a small, picturesque community. It is a fishing village where boat-building is still carried on. There is a Post Office, a telephone station and a few shops. A monument to the fishermen of Cherokee was built by the local community and gives information on local Cherokee heroes.

Hole-in-the-Wall

On the southern extremity of Abaco stands the **Hole-in-the-Wall Lighthouse** which shows the way into the Providence Channel.

Mainland again

Murphy and Dundas Town, adjacent to Marsh Harbour, combine with it to make the third largest town in The Bahamas. Dundas Town just north of Marsh Harbour, was named after Governor Dundas (Governor of the Bahamas from 1937 to 1940). Murphy Town was established to the north-west of Dundas Town and was named in honour of Sir William Murphy, Governor of The Bahamas from 1945 to 1950. These two communities were settled by residents who lived at Cornish Town and Old Place and who were relocated after the devastating hurricane of 1932.

South of Marsh Harbour lie **Spring City** and **Snake Cay**. These were built by Owen Illinois who had a lumber operation and established a short-lived sugar operation which was abandoned in 1970. Earlier in this century, an American Company established **Wilson City**, a lumber camp, near Spenser's Point. Hardly any trace can be seen of it now. In its heyday, before 1916, the mill produced between 15 and 18 million feet of lumber annually.

Crossing Rocks

On the way south from Marsh Harbour to Sandy Point is Crossing Rocks which is located at a very narrow point of Great Abaco Island. Most people of this small village live by fishing.

Sandy Point

This is the southernmost settlement on Great Abaco. It lies about 40 miles south-west of Marsh Harbour. It is a neat, well-laid-out village, and its inhabitants live mainly from fishing, including crawfishing. There are many boats in evidence which tell of its seafaring existence. It is a very prosperous settlement.

Abaco is a fascinating place – an island of contrasts. Its cays resemble New England villages, while some of its mainland communities have an almost African yard pattern of settlements. The waters and beaches of Abaco are beautiful; the sailing is superb; the fishing thrilling! There is history (visit the two museums), historic houses, shopping, underwater reserves, sport and much more. Moreover, Abaconians are friendly. For action or tranquillity visit the Abacos.

Eleuthera – island of freedom

Introduction
Over 300 years ago English Puritan Adventurers in search of religious freedom discovered Eleuthera. It is not certain where they landed but they founded what was probably the first democracy in the western world.

Eleuthera is an island of contrasts. It is just over a mile wide at most places but is 110 miles long. It has magnificent pink-white beaches, sheltered coves, breathtaking bluffs and cliffs and fine harbours. The cliffs are in the north where the deep blue colour of the Atlantic Ocean can be seen on one side and the calmer turquoise Caribbean Sea on the other. In the centre of the island is the hilly farming area – famous for pineapples and tomatoes. In the south the island is green and flatter with quaint New England-like villages.

Exploring Eleuthera
The North Eleuthera airport is convenient for all the northern settlements including Gregory Town. Local taxi drivers are always willing and eager to take you to your destination.

Perhaps the most desirable places to stay in North Eleuthera are at **Current, Spanish Wells, Harbour Island** and **Gregory Town**.

The Current, North Eleuthera (overleaf)
(DEPARTMENT OF ARCHIVES – GAIL SAUNDERS)

110

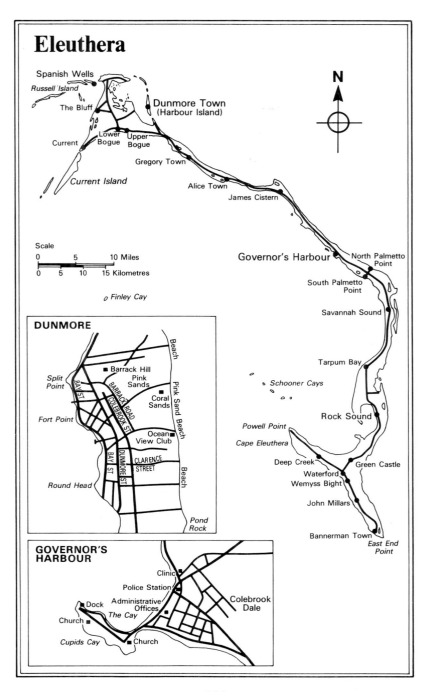

Eleuthera

Spanish Wells

Russell Island

The Bluff

Dunmore Town
(Harbour Island)

Current

Lower Bogue

Upper Bogue

Current Island

Gregory Town

Alice Town

James Cistern

Scale

0   5   10 Miles

0   5   10   15 Kilometres

Finley Cay

Governor's Harbour

North Palmetto Point

South Palmetto Point

Savannah Sound

Tarpum Bay

Schooner Cays

Rock Sound

Powell Point

Cape Eleuthera

Deep Creek

Green Castle

Waterford
Wemyss Bight

John Millars

Bannerman Town

East End Point

DUNMORE

Beach

Split Point

Barrack Hill

Pink Sands

BAY ST

BARRACK ROAD

COLEBROOK ST

Fort Point

Coral Sands

Pink Sand Beach

Ocean View Club

BAY ST

DUNMORE ST

CLARENCE STREET

Beach

Round Head

Pond Rock

GOVERNOR'S HARBOUR

Clinic

Police Station

Administrative Offices

Colebrook Dale

Dock

The Cay

Church

Cupids Cay

Church

Current

Current gets its name from the tide which runs through **The Cut** and which separates it from Current Island. The settlement at Current is small and quaint. The origin of its people is still a mystery. Some say they are descended from the Arawak Indians who comprised the indigenous population before being taken away by the Spaniards. Others think that Current people are descended from American Red Indians. Houses are usually small and painted in pastel colours. The inhabitants fish and farm for a living. There are a few stores and accommodation for tourists is available at **Sea Raiders** and **Sandcastle** small apartment units. Mrs Monica Algreen also offers modest accommodation. There are also facilities for fishing, sailing and watersports.

Excursions in North Eleuthera

Interesting excursions can be made from Current and from the other tourist facilities in North Eleuthera.

Preacher's Cave is a must. It is at this cave that the early Adventurers probably took shelter. It is there they held the first religious service. In 1992, a team of archaeologists and historians from Florida, USA and the Department of Archive in Nassau, discovered artefacts dating back to the mid-seventeenth century. Some skeletons which may also date back to the Puritan Eleutherian Adventurers were also excavated.

The Bluff, a farming community where citrus groves still thrive, has its own dock where the mail-boat docks. Its main families are the Barrys, Hudsons, Dorsetts and Neelys. Besides farming, its inhabitants gather the 'top' from the thatch palms to make straw for the industry which is so popular. Near the Bluff there is a packing house where fruit and vegetables are stored and shipped to Nassau. Bluff does not usually cater for tourists although there is a restaurant, **Arlie's**. There are several well-constructed churches which can be visited in Bluff.

Lower Bogue and **Upper Bogue** are two other settlements which should be visited. Both are farming communities. **Lower Bogue**, which is the larger of the two, also produces masons and carpenters, some of whom work at Spanish Wells. There is a boutique, at least one bar and the **Lady B** restaurant in Lower Bogue. The community exudes prosperity.

Not too far from Lower Bogue is the **Glass Window Bridge**. It is named for the ridge which narrows and almost divides the island into two. Before the bridge was built, the land formed a perfect window in the rock which has been immortalised by the artist Winslow Homer. Today you can still see a smaller window, the original larger one having been washed away in a hurricane. The view of the deep blue ocean and the crashing surf is spectacular.

Before leaving North Eleuthera, even if you do not plan to stay at either place, you must visit **Harbour Island** and **Spanish Wells**.

Harbour Island
From North Eleuthera airport it is a quick ride to the ferry. Speed-boats and a boat-taxi wait to pick up passengers for Harbour Island. It is a delightful ten-minute ride to 'Briland' as its inhabitants affectionately refer to the island. According to the historian, Oldmixon, Harbour Island was named for 'the goodness of the harbour'. It is possible that some of the Eleutherian Adventurers settled here. Among the early settlers were the Russells, Sweetings,

Dunmore Town, Harbour Island – the public dock (GAIL SAUNDERS)

Saunders, Roberts, Pinders, Thompsons, Currys, Barnetts, Alburys, Johnsons and Bethells.

As you approach the island by boat, you can see the picturesque little villages whose houses come down to the shore or the shore road known as Bay Street. 'Briland' is one of the oldest settlements in The Bahamas and once had a population of over a thousand.

Dunmore Town, Harbour Island, has an aura of peacefulness. The settlement was named after the Loyalist Governor, Lord Dunmore, Governor of The Bahamas between 1786-1797. It was at Harbour Island that Dunmore laid out the town and built a modest summer residence. The Commissioner's Residence, built in the early 1920s, now stands on the site of Dunmore's residence. The present building is pleasing to the eye and the grounds are finely manicured.

Harbour Island is one of the most popular resort islands in The Bahamas. Visitors keep coming back year after year. Accommodation ranges in standards of comfort and exclusiveness. The oldest hotel/villa complex on the island is the quaint and quite exclusive **Pink Sands Club** with its individual villas run by the Malcolms. Nearby is the more casual but comfortable **Coral Sands Hotel**. Like Pink Sands it faces on to the three-mile strip of Pink Sand Beach with magnificent views. The cuisine is superb and there is a night-

The Commissioner's Residence, Harbour Island (GAIL SAUNDERS)

club in the park. Other hotels on the beach-side include **Dunmore Beach Club** with cottage accommodation, **Ocean View Club** and the elegant **Runaway Hill Club**. Runaway is small, but each room is large with a private bath. Although almost hidden in a grove of casuarina trees, it is on a bluff that overlooks the spectacular Atlantic Ocean. It also has a swimming pool.

On the harbour side of the island is **Rock House**, a small intimate and exclusive resort hotel with only six guest rooms, and **Romora Bay Club** which, though small, has very comfortable villas, gourmet food, a tennis court and specialises in watersports, especially diving. It is popular with families who can enjoy a variety of activities during the day and meet in the intimate and historic dining room in the evening. Amenities also include a waterfront bar, which serves exotic drinks, and in the winter months a band plays at least once a week. Here you can dance under the stars. **Valentine's Yacht Club and Inn** also faces the harbour. It has 21 rooms but still manages to combine intimacy with an air of luxury and comfort. It has a marina, yacht club, scuba-diving centre and a new spa facility. The **Pink Sand Beach** is only a few minutes walk away. If you do not stay there, at least taste one of their gourmet lunches or dinners. Remember to make reservations for dinner at all the hotels.

Neither on the Bay or the beach-side is **Tingum Village**, run by the Percenti family of Harbour Island. Besides getting a good clean and comfortable room, you can eat at the restaurant there which serves tasty local foods.

There are other small restaurants like **Angela's** where you can get a boiled fish and grits breakfast, lunch and dinner. A variety of small bars and clubs are all within walking distance of the hotels.

Several gift shops, including **Frank's Art Gallery**, sell a variety of Bahamian souvenirs. Straw work can be purchased on Bay Street at **Alvina's** and **Curlene's**.

Although the island is small there is much to do. Fishing is good and local guides are available. Snorkelling is superb at the nearby reefs. There is also water-skiing and scuba-diving.

You can learn a great deal by just wandering around this historic settlement. **Barrack's Hill** past the Cricket Ground was once the site of a military barracks built by Lord Dunmore. The **Methodist Church** on Dunmore and Chapel Road is a magnificent structure. Built in 1840, it shows how large the Methodist congregation was at that time. Just across from the Methodist Church is **Temperance**

Square, a memorial to Thomas Johnson, MD, born in 1837. He was one of the first Harbour Islanders to qualify as a doctor and to return home to serve his people. The Methodist Manse is on Dunmore and Church Streets. Nearly opposite the manse is the **St John's Anglican Church**, originally established in 1768, which is one of the oldest foundations in The Bahamas. The Bell Tower was erected in 1860 and the church was extended in 1888. The Roman Catholic Church, **St Benedict's**, is nearby as is the Convent which was built to house the Sisters of Charity who arrived on the island in 1922. Further along on Dunmore Street is the **Sir George Roberts Memorial Library**. This is a modern building, having been erected in April 1966 to the memory of Harbour Islander Sir George Roberts who served as a Member of the House of Assembly, a Member of the Executive Council, President of the Legislative Council and the Senate. The Library is on the site of an old cemetery once known as 'Up Yonder'.

On Bay Street are **Hill Steps**, which were cut out by prisoners. It is said than an underground tunnel leads from **Picaroon Cove** near the steps to Rock House.

Any visitor to Harbour Island will realise that the old colonial-style architecture on the island has been preserved. Many of the wooden or clapboard houses with decorative fretwork date back to 1790. Harbour Island is known for its quaint architecture, its fine houses with balconies, picket fences, lattice work, dormer windows and garrets.

Titus Hole, a cave with an open mouth that overlooks the harbour and is said to be the first jail of Harbour Island, is well worth a visit. **Fort Point Cottage** commemorates the victory of the 'old heads' of Harbour Island over the Spaniards.

When you become tired of sports and sightseeing you can wander down to **The Fig Tree** on the Bay and just sit, catch the breeze and hear the old heads of 'Briland' tell their exciting tales of adventure.

Spanish Wells

Spanish Wells is also approached by ferry boat. At **Gene's Bay**, the 'Midnight Rider' and other boats are waiting to take visitors over.

Spanish Wells got its name from the days when the Spanish galleons sailed the waters of what was then known as St George's Cay in the sixteenth century. The Spaniards dug large fresh-water wells – hence the name **Spanish Wells**.

Most of the inhabitants of Spanish Wells can trace their roots back to the Eleutherian Adventurers. They are a fiercely proud people, independent and hard-working. For over three hundred years they have been making their living from the sea. They are renowned as fishermen and in recent years have become wealthy on crawfishing – so much so, that Spanish Wells has been called 'the island crawfish built'. Spanish Wellians are also excellent pilots and fishing guides and the waters around Spanish Wells are famous for big game-fishing.

The island is also a yachting centre with fine marina facilities. There are only two tourist facilities on the island, both under the same management. The **Spanish Wells Beach Resort** faces a shallow blue-green sea which laps the white sand beach. Its 21 rooms and 7 cottages all face the sea and are sheltered by shady tropical trees. From this serene and friendly resort you can swim, scuba-dive, fish, water-ski, snorkel or just lounge on the powdery sand beach. An extensive menu is offered in the restaurant.

Across the island is the **Harbour Club** which also offers spacious and comfortable rooms complete with a panoramic view of the harbour. This facility is the home of the Spanish Wells diving centre and offers daily reef trips, specialising in scuba-diving and rental equipment.

Besides watersports you can explore the one-and-three-quarter mile length and half-mile width of the island which has a four-mile perimeter road. The island is divided in two parts. The Old Town (i.e. the east side) has ancient clapboard houses with 'gingerbread house' decorations and lovely gardens full of flowering trees. Its streets are narrow and cobbled. In the western section, the houses are mainly cement-block houses, often large, on spacious, well-manicured lots with small fruit gardens and satellite dishes. The island is said to have 500 cars and 400 motorcycles, mainly of Japanese manufacure. There are no sidewalks – everyone drives. Wellsmen keep spotless homes and gardens and never lock doors. There is no serious crime.

Facilities are modern and you can eat at the six restaurants and a snack bar (this is closed between 1 p.m. and 5 p.m.). After sundown the action is usally to be found at the **Yacht Haven** or **The Cave**. Pool is played at the latter to the sound of jukebox music. There are also dining rooms at the two hotels. Other amenities include two food stores, a clinic, a Government complex, a school, a public park and several stores, including one for straw and quilts run by the Pinder sisters who meet daily to hand-stitch the quilts.

Three churches exist for the very hardworking and God-fearing Wellsmen – the People's Church, the Methodist Church and the Gospel Chapel. On Sundays and some week-nights, pews are packed. All are well kept as is the whole pristine settlement of Spanish Wells. The Spanish Wells Museum, which was opened on 28 December, 1991, is located in an ancient wooden house which was restored by Marvin and Nancy Pinder. It is a treat, containing photographs and artefactual exhibits of the early history of Spanish Wells and the surrounding area. It highlights local crafts such as quilting, also the Lucayans and Eleutherian Adventurers. There is a Lucayan canaye, a garden of local trees and an old outside oven. A gift shop is situated at the rear of the museum.

Gregory Town

Gregory Town, also in North Eleuthera, is famous for its sweet pineapples which are grown in the deep rich soil. It is a hilly, picturesque village with lovely pastel-coloured cottages which mostly overlook the sparkling blue-watered harbour which pirates called 'The Cove'. It is at Gregory Town that the Atlantic waves crash against the shore and provide some of the best surfing in the area.

You can stay right at the northern end of Gregory Town at the modest but clean **Cambridge Villas**. Here there is a restaurant which serves delicious Bahamian food and has a swimming pool. North of Gregory Town is the more luxurious, though reasonably priced, **Oleander Gardens**, in forty acres overlooking the beautiful Atlantic with its own private beach and excellent amenities. Finely decorated and elegantly furnished villas are available for everyone, particularly suitable for families or couples – quiet, restful and serene. Available are a tennis court, fine fishing and watersports, including sailing, snorkelling and wind-surfing. There is also free daily bus transportation for shopping at nearby Gregory Town, or for fishing trips and excursions. Self-drive cars are available upon request. The taxi-fare from North Eleuthera airport is approximately $20.00. There are several interesting gift shops in Gregory Town which sell locally-made arts and crafts.

Hatchet Bay

Driving into Hatchet Bay from Gregory Town you will see what remains of the once thriving plantation established in the 1950s. Silos where feed was once stored for the cattle still stand. The Hatchet Bay Plantation, which is being partially revived, was once the biggest dairy and poultry farm in The Bahamas. **The Cave** is on the way and is worth a visit. It is about a mile long and has the most beautiful stalagmites and stalactites which appear as 'underground cathedrals' in the light.

James Cistern
Before Governor's Harbour Airport is James Cistern, a quiet fishing village which hugs the coast. Here, apparently, young men of fifteen begin building the house to which they will bring their brides. As each man earns a little money, he adds to it.

Governor's Harbour
Governor's Harbour, one of the oldest, if not the oldest settlement in The Bahamas, is an excellent place to stay, being located in the middle of Eleuthera. It is on a high ridge which slopes down into the magnificent sheltered harbour. Opposite the ridge across the harbour is **Cupid's Cay**, said to be the original settlement in Governor's Harbour. The cay is picturesque and the stately house of the commissioner is to be found there. It is connected to the mainland of Governor's Harbour by a causeway. On the way back from the quaint settlement on the cay you will pass a very old Anglican Church, **St Patrick's**, and the **Government complex** which is painted a pretty pastel pink.

There are some small guest houses but among the more comfortable and popular hotels is the **Buccaneer Hill Club**, which has an excellent view of Cupid's Cay and the town. It has a bar and a lively atmosphere. Nearby is **Cigatoo** (the Arawak Indian name for Eleuthera) **Inn** which is also equipped with modern amenities, including a swimming pool, bar and restaurant.

On the ridge on the ocean side of Governor's Harbour is **Club Mediterranée**, the original location of French Leave. This French-based operation is a vacation village where all types of entertainment are arranged. The atmosphere is informal and friendly and most meals are buffet-style. Swimming and tennis are favourite sports.

The sun sets over Cupid's Cay, Governor's Harbour (overleaf)
(GAIL SAUNDERS)

A few miles from the vacation village there is a marina and water-sports centre. Club Med, with its lovely sandy beaches, wooden walkways, cliffs, tropical flowers and plants is a perfect place for a family holiday.

Also available for visitors to Governor's Harbour are **Palmetto Shore Villas** and **Rainbow Inn**.

In Governor's Harbour itself, you can browse at several gift shops including **Norma's** where fine Bahamian batiks and other souvenirs are sold. You should also wander over to **Donell's** for fabrics, ceramics and other gifts. A straw market exists and several restaurants such as **Blue Room**, a well kept, basic restaurant where local fare is offered at reasonable prices. The **Blue Room** also has a billiard table.

Just outside Governor's Harbour are two restaurants, **Blue Waters** and **Kohinoor**.

In town there is the Bayfront Plaza, a shopping centre where banking facilities can be found. In contrast to these modern concrete structures are the fine old clapboard homes on the hill. Many of these, including the **Pyfrom House**, with its 'gingerbread' decorations, dormer windows and typical railed porches, can be seen. Governor's Harbour truly has an air of old world charm.

Going south

South of Governor's Harbour are two small communities, **North Palmetto Point** which boasts a huge 120-year-old silk cotton tree, and **South Palmetto Point** which used to specialise in bonefishing. The quaint small village of **Savannah Sound** is further south. It was renowned for its bread, baked in a huge outdoor oven.

Eighteen miles from Governor's Harbour is **Windermere Island**, an exclusive resort which is often frequented by members of the Royal Family, especially Prince Charles and Princess Diana. The late Earl Mountbatten of Burma used to visit Windermere Island every year and introduced Prince Charles to it. The infamous picture of the Princess in her bikini on the pink sand beach of Windermere Island caused an international sensation.

To get to Windermere Island you have to cross a small bridge and pass through a security gate. Security is particularly tight when any of the Royal Family are staying in one of the villas. The island is narrow with a lovely beach, thatched cabanas and has beautifully manicured gardens around its homes. There is also the exclusive

Windermere Island Club which is tastefully decorated. Here, the visitor can wind-surf, sail-fish, swim or just stroll. Besides the Prince and Princess, visitors might come across other well-known people.

Further south is **Tarpum Bay**, a quaint, tranquil village with a pretty cove and pastel-coloured cottages hugging its shores. It is renowned for the art gallery where a Scotsman, Macmillan Hughes, exhibited steel sculptures and water colours. Accommodation is available at **Hilton Haven** and **Cartwright's Villas**, which are modest but comfortable.

Continuing south you will come to **Rock Sound**, the largest town on Eleuthera. It is the business centre of south Eleuthera and at one time was called 'Wreck Sound' after the pastime or industry of wrecking practised by its inhabitants. One sight that should not be missed is the famous landlocked ocean hole in the town which is said to be over 100 fathoms deep. One of the best places to stay is the **Cotton Bay Club** which has an eighteen-hole golf course. There is the beach and other watersports for the non-golfer.

Further south are the farming villages of **Green Castle, Wemyss Bight** and **Bannerman Town. Davis Harbour** was built as a boating centre and has a good marina. At **Powell Point** on the south-western shore of the island is **Cape Eleuthera** which is now closed, but which is being developed by Landquest International Ltd. It was built with facilities for tennis, golf and swimming. It also has an excellent marina facility. There is a clubhouse with a bar and dining room.

Andros – 'the big yard'

Introduction

Andros is the largest island in The Bahamas being about 104 miles long and 40 miles wide. It lies in the Atlantic Ocean and is made up of many islets and cays comprising a North, Middle and Southern Bight. There is, however, much shallow water and swamp. Some of the swamps connect with fresh water streams and Andros is known for its abundant fresh water supplies. The island has a good deal of hardwood such as mahogany, lignum vitae (the national tree of The Bahamas) and mastic which are used in the building of boats. There are also extensive forests of pine.

Andros has an atmopshere about it – one of mystery. Having many

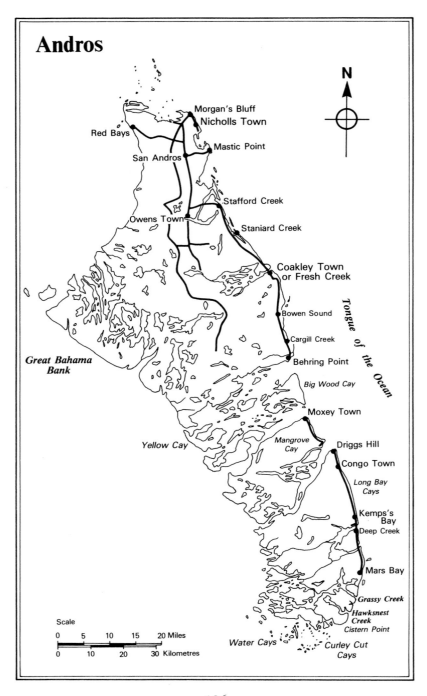

Andros

Morgan's Bluff
Nicholls Town
Red Bays
Mastic Point
San Andros
Stafford Creek
Owens Town
Staniard Creek
Coakley Town
or Fresh Creek
Bowen Sound
Tongue of the Ocean
Cargill Creek
Behring Point
Great Bahama Bank
Big Wood Cay
Moxey Town
Mangrove Cay
Driggs Hill
Yellow Cay
Congo Town
Long Bay Cays
Kemps's Bay
Deep Creek
Mars Bay
Grassy Creek
Hawksnest Creek
Cistern Point
Water Cays
Curley Cut Cays

Scale

| 0 | 5 | 10 | 15 | 20 Miles |

| 0 | 10 | 20 | 30 Kilometres |

forested and remote areas, legend has it that a sort of pixie, leprechaun or gremlin known locally as the 'chickcharney' holds sway. The chickcharnies are thought to be small birdlike beings with large eyes, which, when not up to mischief, rest in the pine trees. Myth has it that these animals migrated with the Seminole Indians in the nineteenth century. Locals believe that it is unwise to irritate a chickcharney; retribution lies in store for anyone who does them wrong. The story goes that a Mr Neville Chamberlain, who managed his father's sisal plantation near Mastic Point, Andros in the 1890s, suffered failure because he cut so many trees down.

History

The island was given the name 'La Isla del Espirito Santo', the Island of the Holy Spirit, by the Spaniards. On a 1782 map, however, it was called San Andreas. The modern name is believed to be in honour of Sir Edmund Andros, Commander of His Majesty's Forces in Barbados in 1672 and Governor successively of New York, Massachusetts, Virginia and Maryland. Sir Edmund was connected with the families of the Lords Proprietors Craven and Carteret. It is possible that the island could also have been named after the inhabitants of St Andro Island on the Mosquito Coast – about 1,400 of them were settled in Andros in 1787.

Loyalists and their slaves also settled in Andros in the late nineteenth century. Many acres of land were cleared and some cotton was grown. Later a sisal plantation was established near Mastic Point in the 1890s.

Sponging was a flourishing industry in Andros for many years. More than half of the male population, including some schoolboys, were involved in the industry until its demise in 1938 when a fungus hit the sponge beds.

Farming has always been practised on Andros. Crops such as corn, peas, bananas, cassava, sweet potatoes and sugar-cane were grown, mainly for domestic use.

Andros as a tourist centre

Only twenty miles west of Nassau, the capital of The Bahamas, Andros is easily reached by airplane. The four airfields are located at San Andros (in the north), Andros Town and Mangrove Cay (central Andros) and Congo Town (in the south). Additionally, there are three official ports of entry – Fresh Creek (central), Congo Town

A seagull, commonly known as a laughing gull (LISA ADDERLEY)

(south), and Mastic Point (north) – which service boats, aircraft and seaplanes.

North Andros
Nicholl's Town with a settlement of about 600 people is the main commercial and tourist centre in the north. At this settlement there is the Commissioner's Office, a clinic with a resident nurse and a telephone station. **The Andros Beach Hotel**, well known as the home of Neal Watson's Andros Undersea Adventurers, is at the northern edge of Nicholl's Town. There are several nightclubs and restaurants in Nicholl's Town on San Andros. The *Yachtsman's Guide* recommends **Eva's Picaroon Restaurant** in Nicholl's Town.

Near to Nicholl's Town is **Morgan's Bluff**, said to be named after the pirate Sir Henry Morgan who hid as-yet-undiscovered treasure there.

To the west of Nicholl's Town is **Red Bay**, a remote village settled by Seminole/Negroes fleeing from the United States in 1821. For many years, the village lay isolated and could only be reached by boat. The descendants of the original settlers continued to practise some of their traditional crafts, such as basket-weaving, and it has been said that they lived together as a 'tribe'.

At the fascinating village of **San Andros** you will be amazed by the changing landscapes, the huge pine trees, the hidden lakes and the blue holes.

A drive south along the coast road will take you past **Stafford Creek**, a small settlement strung out along the north side of an inlet. **Staniard Creek** is the next major settlement. It has fairly good anchorage, lovely beaches and lots of casuarinas.

Central Andros

About nine miles south of Staniard Creek are **Fresh Creek** and **Coakley Town**, small settlements on the north shore. Just north of Coakley Town is **Small Hope Bay Lodge** which, since 1960,

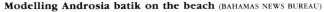

Modelling Androsia batik on the beach (BAHAMAS NEWS BUREAU)

has been a popular dive resort. Founded by Canadian Dick Birch, Small Hope Bay Lodge has comfortable cabins of island rock and pine. There is a large central dining room which sometimes comes alive with impromptu entertainment.The beach is inviting and, for the more intrepid scuba-divers, equipment is provided for daily tours to the beautiful Tongue of the Ocean reefs.

Nearby in Fresh Creek is the unique **Androsia** factory. Established by Rosi Birch, Androsia is run by the Birch family and produces batik with exquisite local designs. Rosi Birch's cottage industry used Indonesian methods which means that fabric is handpainted and dyed. Androsia is sold all over The Bahamas and now has an international market. Its lovely colours – pinks, purples, blues, yellows – and its unique patterns – flowers, fish, butterflies – captivate nearly all visitors to The Bahamas who are more than likely to wear at least one Androsian outfit. Most batiks are on cotton, but some silk patterns are also produced.

Andros Town or **Fresh Creek** is a picturesque settlement. A modest Lifestyle Museum has been established by the Andros Branch of the Bahamas Historical Society in Fresh Creek. It is the main population centre in central Andros. There is Papa Gay's **Chickcharnie Hotel** with its comfortable rooms and which serves delicious Bahamian meals. Her Majesty the Queen visited Fresh Creek in October 1985. This was her first visit to any of the Family Islands. She also toured AUTEC (Atlantic Undersea Test and Evaluation Centre), a US/Bahamian collaborative venture for underwater testing. It is one of the best and busiest underwater testing facilities in the world. The area is off-limits to yachtsmen. The Queen's visit helped to bring Andros to the forefront and during her visit the former Prime Minister, Sir Lynden Pindling, (the Member of Parliament for Kemp's Bay) announced great development plans for Andros.

Small settlements to the south such as **Bowen Sound, Cargill Creek** and **Behring Point** hug the coast. These are not tourist resorts but are worth seeing for their beaches, coconut palms and wooded shorelines.

South of these are the Bights of Andros – Northern Bight, Middle Bight and Southern Bight. Between these Bights, lying among the creeks, are many cays. The largest of these cays is **Mangrove Cay** with its main settlement running along the coast. Areas in the settlement are named after prominent families, such as Pinders,

Dorsets, Peats and Swains. Bahamasair, the national flag-carrier, lands at Moxey Town, named after a Ragged Island family who settled there. In **Moxey Town** there is a comfortable guest-house operated by Hubert and Katrina King. Delicious Bahamian dishes are prepared by Mrs King.

Mangrove Cay, which has lovely beaches, lagoons, coconut trees, vegetation and caves, is the site of a colourful three-day August Monday Regatta when Bahamian sailors have a chance to test their sailing skills.

Further south is **Lisbon Creek**, a scenic settlement known for its boat-building. Excellent Bahamian sloops have been built here and many have distinguished themselves in the Family Island Regatta. Three well known boat-builders are Alfred Bain, Bernard Longley and Leroi Bannister.

Accommodation is available at **Longley House** or **Bannister House**, also known for tasty Bahamian food. A favourite meeting spot is **Leroi's Harbour Bar**.

South Andros

Across the Southern Bight, a very exciting journey by boat, is **Drigg's Hill**. About two miles south of Drigg's Hill, on the shore near **Congo Town** is the **Emerald Palms Hotel**, formerly Las Palmas Hotel, which has been extensively renovated and redecorated. It is ideal for honeymooners and is a very peaceful place with a lovely beach and beautiful views. About a mile further south is the **Congo Beach Club**, a guest-house/restaurant located on the beach. Congo Town is the main settlement and is served by Bahamasair.

South of Congo Town on the long but pretty coast road is **High Rock**, known for its decorative wood on the roof-tops, the **Bluff** and **Long Bay Cays**, the birthplace of Lady Pindling, the wife of the former Prime Minister. Another small settlement before reaching **Kemps's Bay,** the site of the Commissioner's Office, is **Smith's Hill**. South of Kemps's Bay is **Deep Creek**, a very picturesque settlement named for the deep creek that separates the larger land-mass of Andros from it. There is now a bridge joining the two sides of the creek. Deep Creek traditionally was known for its fish, conch and crabs. Two settlements lie to the south of Deep Creek, **Little**

Emerald palms near Congo Town, South Andros (overleaf)
(EMERALD PALMS HOTEL)

Creek and **Mars Bay**. Fishing is excellent in these parts and it is fun to explore the usually shallow creeks by dinghy.

The Berry Islands

Just 19 miles east of Bimini and 30 miles from Nassau are the Berry Islands, a chain of about 30 small islands. Only about 500 people live permanently in the Berrys and most are settled at **Bullocks Harbour** on **Great Harbour Cay**.

Being located on the edge of the Tongue of the Ocean, the Berrys are popular with divers, anglers and yachtsmen.

It is believed that the Berrys were first settled in 1836 when Governor Colebrooke established a settlement of liberated Africans at **Great Harbour Cay**, the largest of the Berry Islands. Sparse soil and the scarcity of water made it difficult to make a living from farming.

Some years ago, a resort with excellent marina and hotel/villa facilities existed at Great Harbour Cay. Today, this resort is closed. However, there are gas and fuel facilities, a telephone station and a clinic at Great Harbour Cay.

At the southern end of the chain is **Chub Cay** which has a semi-private resort, the **Chub Cay Club**. The latter has been described as beautiful and offers fine accommodation. On the east side of the harbour, it also has a pool. Its restaurant serves excellent Bahamian dishes and the service is professional. Telephone facilities exist at the club.

The Chub Cay Club, which has the advantage of being near the Great Bahama Bank and the Tongue of the Ocean, is renowned as a sport-fishing resort for yachtsmen. It is also popular among sport-divers. **Chub Cay Undersea Adventurers** is a part of the Neal Watson's Family Island dive centres. It provides divers with a variety of interesting dives, including the **Chub Cay Wall** (in 80 feet of water), the **Oasis** (which is known for its large tiger groupers), **Canyons and Caves** (a shallow but beautiful reef in about 20 to 40 feet of water) and **Mamma Rhoda Rock** known for its schools of grunt and the yellow trumpetfish.

At **Great Stirrup Cay** there is a lighthouse which was built in 1863. At this pretty island, cruise ships stop to allow tourists to swim and picnic on the beautiful white sandy beaches.

Between Great Harbour Cay and the Stirrup Cays are a number

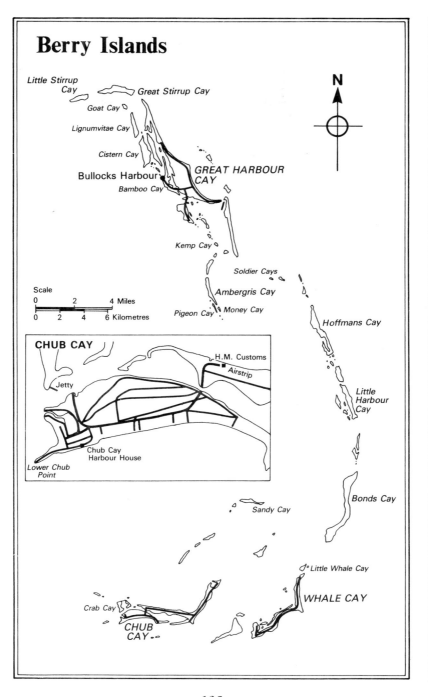

Berry Islands

Little Stirrup Cay

Great Stirrup Cay

Goat Cay

Lignumvitae Cay

Cistern Cay

Bullocks Harbour

GREAT HARBOUR CAY

Bamboo Cay

Kemp Cay

Soldier Cays

Ambergris Cay

Pigeon Cay

Money Cay

Hoffmans Cay

N

Scale

| 0 | 2 | 4 Miles |
| 0 | 2 | 4 | 6 Kilometres |

CHUB CAY

H.M. Customs

Airstrip

Jetty

Little Harbour Cay

Chub Cay Harbour House

Lower Chub Point

Bonds Cay

Sandy Cay

Little Whale Cay

WHALE CAY

Crab Cay

CHUB CAY

of privately owned cays. These include **Bird Cay**, which features tall casuarinas, citrus and coconut groves and a number of luxurious homes, gardens and public buildings. In the southern part of the chain, **Whale Cay** is in the process of being developed. Plans include a 3000-foot airstrip and a protected marina. **Frozen and Alder's Cays**, which are almost joined together, are a paradise for bird-watchers and nature lovers. **Little Harbour Cay**, according to the 1987 *Yachtsman's Guide to The Bahamas* is one of the 'prettiest harbours in the Berry Islands'. On **Little Whale Cay**, formerly owned by the late Wallace Groves founder of Freeport, Grand Bahama, there is an airstrip, harbour and a well-landscaped private residence. It is a private island, and landing is not permitted.

Bimini – Hemingway's retreat

Just 50 miles from Florida is Bimini, known for its 'big-game fishing', uncrowded beaches, diving and partying night-life. Chalk's Airlines flies amphibious planes from Nassau and Miami and the trips themselves are scenic ones. Bimini today is a tourist centre with fine hotels and marine facilities.

History

There are two main islands which make up Bimini, North Bimini and South Bimini. North Bimini has most of the population and has traditionally been the place to live. South Bimini was used mainly for farming.

Bimini has had an exciting past. It was a 'rendezvous' for wreckers who, it is believed, eventually settled in the islands in the mid-nineteenth century. When the erection of the lighthouses brought a halt to wrecking, the people of Bimini tried fishing, sponging and growing sisal and coconuts. When Prohibition was declared in the United States, Bimini became an entrepôt for the rum-runners. After the repeal of the Volstead Act, Biminites began to cater to wealthy fishermen who realised that Bimini offered some of the best fishing grounds in the world.

One such person was Ernest Hemingway who discovered Bimini in the summer of 1935. Hemingway engaged in sport-fishing or big-game fishing in Bimini for a number of years. He also frequented its bars, generally enjoyed himself, and wrote. His novel *Islands in the Stream* captured his impression of Bimini and also his battle to

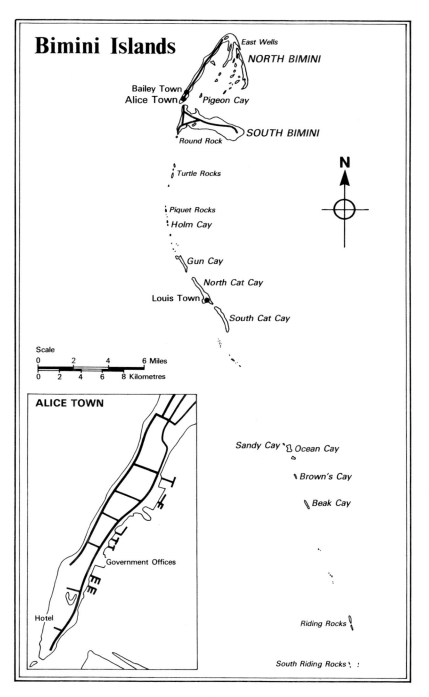

Bimini Islands

East Wells

NORTH BIMINI

Bailey Town
Alice Town
Pigeon Cay

SOUTH BIMINI

Round Rock

Turtle Rocks

N

Piquet Rocks
Holm Cay

Gun Cay

North Cat Cay

Louis Town

South Cat Cay

Scale

| 0 | 2 | 4 | 6 Miles |
| 0 | 2 | 4 | 6 | 8 Kilometres |

ALICE TOWN

Sandy Cay Ocean Cay

Brown's Cay

Beak Cay

Government Offices

Hotel

Riding Rocks

South Riding Rocks

catch large fish in the Gulf Stream. He and Adam Clayton Powell are two celebrities who are remembered by old-timers in Bimini.

North Bimini

As you enter Bimini's Harbour where Chalk's Airline operates you will find that there are many places to anchor. There is **Captain Harcourt Brown's Hotel and Marina** which has space for 30 boats. In addition it has all marine services, a restaurant and 'lively' bar. Next to Brown's is **Freddy Weech's Bimini Dock** which can accommodate up to 15 boats. Further north is **Bimini's Blue Water Marina**, a fine, popular docking spot which has space for 32 yachts. It supplies marine and fishing services and has accommodation on shore. Then there is the **Big Game Fishing Club** which offers fishing and scuba services. The club boasts a good restaurant and bar and also has crafts, jewellery and liquor shops. The Big Game Club is the headquarters for BASRA (Bahamas Air Sea Rescue Association) in Bimini.

On shore is Alice Town, the foremost settlement in Bimini, whose main street, **King's Highway**, is a narrow road lined with bars and shops. At one end of Kingsway is a monument, an arched concrete 'gateway to The Bahamas'. On the Highway, most of the buildings are pastel coloured. There are numerous liquor stores, bars, grocery shops, a bakery, a laundromat, a public library, a Post Office, a bank and a church. There is also a newly-constructed Government complex. Estelle Rolle's raisin bread and coconut rolls are a must.

Among the more popular places to visit are **Captain Bob's Conch Hall of Fame** for a coffee and take-out lunches, **The End of the World War** for a drink and to wait for friends, and the **Red Lion Pub and Restaurant** which offers delicious seafood and a place to watch 'Bimini parade by'.

Perhaps one of the most interesting places is the **Compleat Angler Hotel**, built in the 1930s and where Ernest Hemingway stayed. The hotel is well known for its collection of Hemingway memorabilia. Its bar, with its dark panelled walls and numerous photographs and artefacts, mostly relating to Hemingway, really comes alive after dinner. It is probably best to visit the library early, before the place begins to hop with loud calypso and rock music. Another nightspot is the **Hy Star Disco**.

On the main street there are also many small shops which sell T-shirts, jewellery, imported perfume, straw goods and the like. One tiny shop, **Wicks and Sticks**, sells lamps constructed of popsicle sticks. There is also a bookstore which sells newspapers, magazines, guide books and several books on Bahamian history.

At the highest point on the island is the **Anchorage**, a 'New England' structure which was once the home of the Lerners who built the Lerner Marine Laboratory in Alice Town in the late 1940s. A branch of the American Museum of Natural History, the laboratory was a popular centre for the study of sharks, dolphins, other fish and marine life. It closed its doors in 1974.

There is a fine beach on the western side of Alice Town. At the Anchorage, on the deep-water side, the beach and the water are particularly inviting.

Within walking distance of Alice Town is **Bailey Town**, the residential section of North Bimini. It is a prosperous settlement with many new houses, cars, bicycles and motorbikes. There is an interesting Anglican Church, dedicated to **Our Lady and St Stephen**.

A boat ties up to a small wooden pier in Bimini
(BAHAMAS NEWS BUREAU)

Big-game fishing

Bimini is famous for its big-game fishing – the aim is to catch the heaviest marlin, sail-fish, grouper, wahoo, tuna and more. You can rent a boat with a captain and crew in Alice Town. It is best to do this as they know the waters and can also assist you with your tackle and technique. Fishing tournaments are held from March until August. The season for blue-fin (giant) tuna is between 7 May and 15 June. Blue marlin usually run between June and July and white marlin in the winter and spring.

South Bimini

South Bimini is much quieter than its hectic neighbour, North Bimini. In the south, some farming is still done and there are a few vacation homes. It is South Bimini which legend has it that was explored by Ponce de Leon in search of the sought after 'fountain of youth'. Some have attributed healing powers to the pool there called **Healing Hole**.

Diving

For scuba-divers, check with **Neal Watson's Bimini Undersea Adventurers**. This company arranges dive and accommodation packages at Brown's Hotel and the Big Game Club. Bimini's waters are clear and there are many popular diving spots such as **Rainbow Reef**, a relatively shallow dive, and **Hawksbill Reef**, with waters 45-55 feet deep and lovely coral heads and lobsters. To the south, about an hour's ride from Bimini, there are the **Victory Rocks**, a reef which runs for about four miles.

Gun Cay

About nine miles south of Bimini Harbour is **Gun Cay**, known for its fishing and also the wreck of a concrete ship. The ship, said to be left from the First World War, served as a rum-runner's storehouse during Prohibition. It was said that Bahamian schooners owned by licensed liquor dealers in Nassau anchored inside the cays. Liquor was also stored on the concrete boat and was sold to rum-runners who smuggled it into the United States.

Cat Cay

Not far from Gun Cay, about one mile to the south-east, is Cat Cay, a private club, but still a port of entry for The Bahamas. Visiting yachtsmen can tie up there and a restaurant, bar, laundry facilities and showers are available.

Founded in 1931 by the late Louis Wasey as a secluded get-away for himself and a few friends, Cat Cay is still an exclusive and idyllic hideaway for the likes of the Dupont heirs and their friends.

Ocean Cay

Boaters who go to the southern end of the Bimini chain will see Ocean Cay where aragonite, a pure limestone, is dredged from the bottom of the ocean. Various items such as cement, fertilisers, glass and other products are made from aragonite.

Exumas – yachting mecca and regatta site

The cays

Some have said that the Exumas are the loveliest part of The Bahamas. The Exuma chain should not be missed by the serious visitor. The 360 or so cays, which stretch for about 130 miles

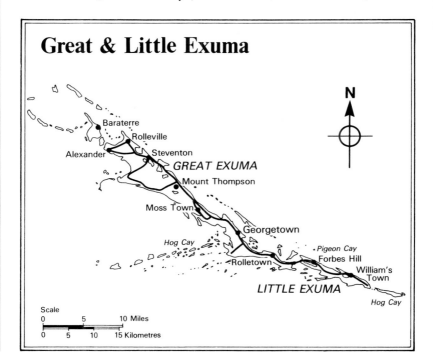

Great & Little Exuma

beginning 30 miles to the south-east of Nassau, are a haven for yachtsmen. On these isolated cays can be found fine anchorages and landlocked harbours. Some islands are tiny with small beaches and a few trees; some rise to green heights; others have rocky cliffs. The crystal clear blue-green waters are breathtaking and excellent for swimming. The beaches and the sea of a large part of the Exuma Cays are being preserved by the Government under The Bahamas National Trust's Exuma National Land and Sea Park. Much of it comprises underwater limestone and coral reefs, drop-offs, blue holes, caves and fantastically beautiful marine life. The park is also renowned for being the last home of the Bahamian iguana which resembles a giant lizard and which once formed part of the Bahamian diet. The park is worth a visit, but can only be approached by boat. Equipment can be rented in George Town or Staniel Cay. In the park, no hunting, spear-fishing or coral collecting is allowed.

Great Exuma

History
As far as we know, Exuma was not permanently settled until after the American Revolutionary War. Many Loyalists and their slaves chose Exuma as their new home, setting up cotton plantations which flourished for a brief time but soon declined.

The Rolles
Among the Loyalist settlers of Exuma were Denys Rolle and later his son Lord John Rolle who was an absentee plantation owner and never came to The Bahamas. Other Loyalists included Roger and John Kelsall from Georgia and South Carolina, William Moss and Thomas Forbes.

Denys Rolle of Devonshire, England, brought over about 140 slaves and settled on Exuma at the time of the evacuation of East Florida. The first settlements were made at Rolleville and Rolle Town and later at Steventon, Ramsey and Mount Thompson. Cotton plantations did not succeed because of soil exhaustion and the chenille bug. Denys Rolle left The Bahamas and his plantations in charge of an overseer in Exuma and an attorney in Nassau. His son, John, who was raised to the peerage in 1796, inherited his father's lands.

A fine specimen of a Bahamian iguana (LISA ADDERLEY)

Legend has it that Lord Rolle granted his lands to be held in commonage by his former slaves. However, no deed has been found to support this belief. Lord Rolle's will, written three years after Emancipation, directed his executors to sell his property in The Bahamas. It seemed that the Rolle slaves, as part of their resistance to slavery, claimed the land. In 1896, the Commonage Act solved some of their legal problems. Most of the former Rolle slaves adopted the surname Rolle. So you will meet many Rolles in Exuma. Today anyone with that surname, or who is closely related, can build on the Rolle properties.

Elizabeth Harbour and George Town
Elizabeth Harbour, which has a draft of 16 feet, has helped in the development of Great Exuma. The harbour has given excellent protection and probably made Exuma a favourite haunt for pirates. The harbour is such a natural one that at one time it was suggested that **George Town** should be the capital of The Bahamas.

143

In modern times, since the early 1950s, the harbour has been the site of the world renowned **Family Island Regatta** in April. It is a festive event – the race of Bahamian work boats. The regatta lasts three days and is a magnificent sight. George Town comes alive at that time and all accommodation is booked a year in advance for this most popular event.

George Town, a port of entry, is the main settlement of the Exumas. It overlooks the harbour and **Stocking Island** on the north side and also has an inland lake, Lake Victoria. George Town had the major airfield in the Exumas, but the main airport has been built at Moss Town. George Town also has electrical power, a medical clinic, a number of churches and hotels.

At the airport there is a restaurant/bar owned by Kermit Rolle, one of the island's best known entrepreneurs. Kermit Rolle is an all-rounder – a farmer, a taxi-driver and a restaurateur.

George Town is a short but scenic drive from the airport. Near the centre of town is a large tree where straw goods are sold. Nearby

The Peace and Plenty Hotel, Exuma (BAHAMAS NEWS BUREAU)

is the **Government Complex Building** which houses the Commissioner's Office, the Post Office and Court House. To the north of the Government Administration building is **St Andrew's Anglican Church**, a part of which is about 150 years old. It has recently been extended.

A haven for visiting yachtsmen, George Town has many places to stay. The **Peace and Plenty Hotel**, named after the boat which brought Denys Rolle's supplies and building materials to Exuma in the nineteenth century, has an anchorage, and is an old favourite for yachtsmen and the ordinary visitor. Legend has it that the spot on which the hotel is built was once a slave market. It was later the location of a private home and guest-house. The Peace and Plenty today is known for attracting celebrities. It serves good food, has a quaint and historic bar and provides live music several nights a week. Guests who stay there can be transported to Stocking Island to swim during the day. The island was once used for fishing and is now known for its beautiful beaches. There are also sunset cruises on Elizabeth Harbour. The Peace and Plenty Hotel recently opened an extension facility, the **Beach Inn**, situated nearby (just over a mile away) at Bonefish Bay. The inn fronts on a 300-foot stretch of Exuma Beach. The two properties are linked by a shuttle bus. The Beach Inn has sixteen up-scale guest rooms, a bar, a restaurant and an office.

Other well-known hotels are **Pieces of Eight**, not far from the Peace and Plenty, the **Out Island Inn**, which offers cottages off the main lobby and **Marshall's Guest House**. Pieces of Eight is known for its Chinese kitchen, its conch in black bean and garlic sauce and its sweet and sour grouper. John Marshall, the owner of Marshall's Guest House, also has a well-stocked grocery store as does the **Darville Store**. The Out Island Inn is located on a beach west of town and is popular with yachtsmen and those arriving by plane. There are other popular eateries such as **Two Turtle Inn** and **Freda Hall's Take-Away**. John Marshall and his wife also operate the **Town Café** a popular bakery and pastry shop.

Moss Town

North from George Town on a most scenic drive past **Goat Cay** and **Simon's Point** up the coast, bear west inland, and you will

An aerial view of the Bights of Andros (overleaf) (PETER RAMSAY)

soon come to **Moss Town**, a small settlement which has a new airport and the **Central High School** for Exuma located on a high hill. There are a number of churches. The main industry is farming. At Moss Town, in Mr Reuben Bodie's yard, there are three tombs and two graves. The three tombs are marked to the memory of Henderson Ferguson, George Butler and Constance McDonald. One grave is believed to be that belonging to an unnamed slave.

Ramsey's is a small village on the way to **Mount Thompson**, where a packing house is located. Farmers bring their produce to be packed and shipped to Nassau. Mount Thompson lies opposite the **Three Sisters Rock** which was named for three sisters who supposedly drowned there. Just north of the settlement is **Ocean Bight**, which has a beautiful beach.

Off the main road, inland to the west, is **The Forest**. The land was formerly owned by the Bowe family. Much farming was done at this settlement. Tenants of Mr Bowe farmed various pastures and in return gave a percentage of the produce to him. This 'tenant' farming led to some confusion and to the celebrated Bowe case in the 1960s. The tenants at that time made an unsuccessful legal bid for the ownership of the land.

There is a splendid view at **Farmer's Hill**, further north up the coast. It has one of the highest points on Great Exuma. The BATELCO (Bahamas Telecommunications Corporation) scatter system is located there.

Steventon is the next major settlement on the north-eastern coast of Great Exuma. It has a number of churches and a school. A salt pond is located near the settlement. Much farming is carried out at Steventon. Inland to the south-east are Calvin Hill and Richmond Hill, two small farming settlements.

Rolleville, one of the main Rolle settlements, is located near the northern tip of Great Exuma. It is a large settlement situated on a hill overlooking the harbour. Its houses are quaint; some still have thatched roofs. The Rolleville and Steventon slaves joined in Pompey's rebellion in the 1830s. They had developed their own farming (or provision) grounds, tended their animals and spent more time on their own affairs. When they were told they were being moved to another island, they rebelled. Most of the slaves nevertheless took the surname Rolle.

Kermit Rolle's **Hilltop Tavern** is on top of the hill and provides refreshment to travellers and locals alike. It is a favourite night-spot for visitors. There are also several churches including a recently built Church of God of Prophecy. Rolleville is mainly a fishing community.

North of Rolleville is **Baraterre**, a small fishing community. Quite a number of the Exuma cays, including **Farmer's Cay, Staniel Cay** and **Black Point** have substantial settlements. Some, like Staniel, have hotel accommodation and docking facilities.

Going south of George Town

Rolle Town
On an excursion by car south of George Town you will soon approach **Rolle Town**. Formerly one of Lord Rolle's plantations, this village sits atop a hill overlooking the sea. A gatepost which once marked the entrance to the estate still survives. Just off the main road there are three tombs dating back to Loyalist times. On the largest tomb an inscription reads: *Within this tomb interred the body of Ann McKay, the wife of Alexander McKay who departed this life on the 8th November, 1792. Age twenty-six years and their Infant Child*. The land at Rolle Town is held in commonage. It is a farming community and one of the largest onion-growing areas in Exuma.

Hartswell
South of Rolle town is **Hartswell**, a small farming village, originally settled by the Bowe family. It is well known for pigeon peas.

The Ferry
A small bridge links Great Exuma and Little Exuma. Until the mid-1960s a ferry boat was used to convey passengers across the small cut. **The Ferry** is the first settlement on Little Exuma. It is a farming community, though some boat-building used to be done. Some well-known families who live or originated at The Ferry are the Fitzgeralds, Knowles, Dames and Bullards. There is a small Anglican Church, St Christopher's, which was built in 1943 and is attended by the Fitzgerald family who migrated from Ireland many years ago; there is also a Church of God and a Baptist Church. There are beautiful sea views from the hills of the settlement. South of The Ferry is **Pretty Molly Bay** which has magnificent beaches. The **Sand Dollar Beach Club Hotel** overlooks the bay, which is superb for picnics.

Forbes Hill

Forbes Hill is the next settlement. It is a small farming community and was named after the original Forbes family that settled there.

Williams Town

On the way to **Williams Town** is an obelisk on top of a steep hill overlooking Little Exuma's salt pond. In the nineteenth century, this marker guided ships to the spot to pick up the salt which was exported by plantation owners such as the Kelsalls. Salt found its way to Nova Scotia, Canada and to other parts of North America. Today some salt is raked for local consumption.

Williams Town is quite a large settlement with several churches including a newly constructed Anglican Church, St Mary Magdalene, dedicated in late 1986. There is also a Church of God.

In the nineteenth century, much of the land was owned by the Kelsall family, Loyalists from South Carolina and Georgia. The family set up cotton plantations and also raked salt at the nearby pond. John Kelsall owned **The Hermitage Estate** on Little Exuma which is only about a mile south of Williams Town. The estate once had a stock of horses, cattle, mules and numerous slaves. It was considered to be one of the most valuable in The Bahamas.

Today, there are few remains of this once-thriving plantation, which is now owned by the Bowe Family. There is the cottage known as **The Hermitage** or Cotton House, probably a part of the original plantation complex. There is a large tomb about 400 yards from the present Hermitage.

Exuma has beauty – witness the National Land and Sea Park, the isolated sandy cays and the marvellous views from the hills of Rolleville, Rolle Town and The Ferry. Exuma has history, for example the remains of the plantations at Williams Town, the ancient tombs at Rolle Town and at Moss Town. Exuma also offers recreation to swimmers, boaters, fishermen, snorkellers and sailors. The Family Island Regatta is a bonus and a **must** if you visit Exuma in mid-to-late April.

Cat Island – island of superstition

Introduction

Cat Island is perhaps the least-known inhabited island in The

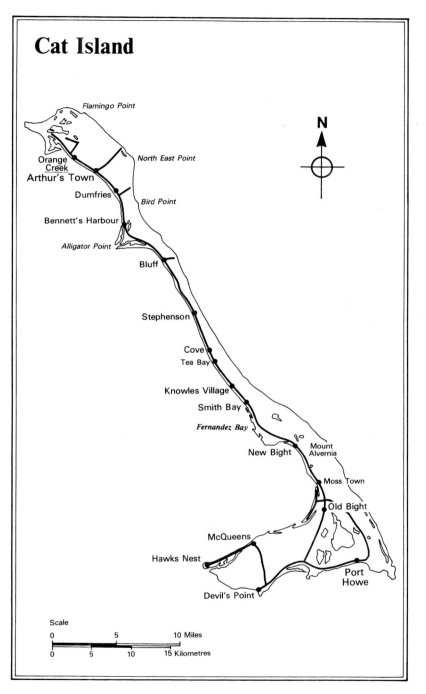

Cat Island

Flamingo Point

Orange Creek
Arthur's Town

North East Point

Dumfries

Bird Point

Bennett's Harbour

Alligator Point

Bluff

Stephenson

Cove
Tea Bay

Knowles Village

Smith Bay

Fernandez Bay

New Bight

Mount Alvernia

Moss Town

Old Bight

McQueens

Hawks Nest

Devil's Point

Port Howe

N

Scale

| 0 | | 5 | | 10 Miles |

| 0 | 5 | 10 | 15 Kilometres |

Bahamas. It is quite beautiful with its rolling hills, especially in the south, and its fantastic empty beaches, especially on the north side. It is a long island, being about 48 miles in length and averaging only one to four miles in width.

The name

No one is certain how it got its name. Some say that it was named for a pirate Arthur Catt who used to frequent the island. For more than four centuries Cat Island was called 'San Salvador' and thought by some to be the first landfall of Columbus in the New World. However, in 1926 Watlings Island (also named after a pirate) was redesignated San Salvador and the name Cat Island was used once again.

Folklore

Cat Island is also known as an 'obeah' island. It is here that the story originated about Sammy Swain, a cripple who fell in love with Belinda, the prettiest girl in the village, and when rebuffed had her 'fixed'. The late musician and composer, Clement Bethel, popularised this tale in his folk opera musical which was performed for Her Majesty The Queen in 1985 when she visited Nassau for the meeting of the Commonwealth Heads of Government. There are many tales of illness, retribution and 'fixes' meted out by the workers of obeah. It is believed that some farmers station 'duppies' in their fields to stop theft. It is not untypical to see trees with bottles filled with dirt, hair and fingernails to protect the owner's property from thieves.

History

The first settlement of any consequence made at Cat Island was in the year 1783 when the Loyalists arrived. Such names as Hepburn, Deveaux, McDonald, Campbell and Sutherland are among those of the early settlers.

Plantations were set up and the ruins of some can still be seen today. After the failure of cotton proprietors and after the abolition of slavery, the freed slaves turned to farming peas, corn, potatoes, cassava and later, in the nineteenth century, to growing pineapples. Today Cat Islanders are still known for their farming. Many islanders still use the slash and burn method to clear the ground of the undergrowth. Some farmers, including women and children, walk miles to their fields which are usually not visible from the road. Peas, beans, melons, okras, onions, pineapples and potatoes are grown by these intrepid farmers.

Exploring Cat Island

Bahamasair flies into the airport near **Arthur's Town**, in the northern part of Cat Island. One of the largest settlements, it is the most important in the north, having a Commissioner's Office, a telephone station, a number of churches, a library and a Government school. Its claim to fame is that it was the home of **Sidney Poitier**, internationally acclaimed actor who wrote about his boyhood days at Arthur's Town in his autobiography *This Life*. His parents were farmers specialising, at the time of Sidney Poitier's birth, in tomatoes. There are ruins of old houses to be seen on the north side but today the settlement is located on the south side which has a sheltered harbour.

North of Arthur's Town is **Orange Creek**, quite a large settlement, which offers excellent bonefishing among its mangroves. It is also a farming community.

Going south along the main road which runs along the sheltered western coast, you will pass **Dumfries** and **Bennett's Harbour**, known for its lovely harbour, which is about a half-a-mile long, and its creeks which can be explored by dinghy. Further south is **Bluff**, once the wealthiest settlement on the island. It sits on high ground and was originally an estate (where cotton was cultivated) owned by James Hepburn. Today, numbers have dwindled, many of its former population having migrated to the United States or to Nassau. The people who are left live mainly by farming. Constable Wilson some years ago introduced pineapples from Port Howe and has reaped many a crop from the red soil of the bluff.

Drive south to **Carey's, Gaitor's, Industrious Hill** (known for its plaiting), **Stephenson** (with its 'prettys' on its roof tops), **Sawyers** and **Cove**, known for its farming, especially for crops of sweet potatoes, pigeon peas and onion. The road south then leads to **Tea Bay** which hugs the shoreline and has boats, mainly dinghies, parked on the beach beneath coconut palms. On the way to **New Bight**, the capital, is a small guest-house, **The Bridge Inn**. It is run by the Russells. Then you will pass **Bachelor's**, a very small settlement, **Knowles**, which is larger and **Smith Bay** with its several churches, a clinic and dock where eight boats call weekly.

About three miles north of New Bight is **Fernandez Bay Village**, a resort developed by the Armbrister family whose ancestors once ran a slave plantation here. It comprises several guest cottages built of local stone and set among casuarina trees. The efficiency cottages open to the white sands of Fernandez Bay. Bookings must be made for dinner, which is served in the panelled dining room. The Fernandez Bay Village is particularly beautiful at sunset.

New Bight is the centre of Government with the Commissioner's Office, residence, telecommunications and Post Office. It also has

The bell tower and chapel at The Hermitage, Mount Alvernia
(BAHAMAS MINISTRY OF TOURISM)

several grocery stores. Above the village of New Bight, along a road leading through the arched doors of an old church, is **Mount Alvernia**, which at 206 feet is the highest hill in The Bahamas. It is quite a climb but worth it. At the top of the 'mountain' is Father Jerome's 'Hermitage'. In the early part of this century, John Hawkes, originally an architect, came to The Bahamas as an Anglican priest. He built five Anglican churches on Long Island. Later, he was ordained as a Roman Catholic priest and became known as Monsignor Jerome Hawkes. He retired to The Bahamas in 1939 and spent his last years working as a priest, architect and mason. The architect of St Augustine College on New Providence, Fr Hawkes decided to build a hermitage on the highest point at Cat Island, and indeed in The Bahamas, when he lived as 'the Hermit of Cat Island'. The retreat comprised a chapel, a bell tower and living quarters with three very small rooms. At the top of this mountain there is a fantastically beautiful view of the green northern end of the island and the blue seas of The Bight. It is no wonder that Fr Jerome, who died in 1956, instructed that his body be buried on Mount Alvernia in a little cave below his hermitage. It is a serene and lovely spot. The view is breathtaking.

Old Bight, about four miles south of New Bight, has a pretty three-mile beach. There is a clinic with a resident nurse. On the way is **The Village** where W.E. Armbrister, a former planter, had a small factory to process sisal which was cultivated in the late nineteenth century. There are remains of a railroad which carried sisal from the fields to the dockside.

Travelling inland from Old Bight in the 'boot' of Cat Island, the next settlement is **Devil's Point**, a pretty village named for the belief that at this village 'cork did sink and iron did float'. Pastel-coloured houses enhance this community, which still has several thatched cottages.

North of Devil's Point is **McQueen's**, where thatched houses and kitchens with chimneys can still be seen. The quaint houses and old kitchens are made of lime and tabby stone work. People here farm and plait straw.

At the tip of the boot, several miles along the coast road from McQueen's, is **Hawk's Nest Club and Marina**. This is a very comfortable resort equipped with its own airstrip, a hotel, a restaurant, a bar and a small marina.

Another resort some miles from Hawk's Nest Creek is the **Cutlass**

Bay Club near to the small settlements of **Bain Town** and **Zonicle's**. The Cutlass Bay Club has a small hotel and restaurant and also has its own airstrip. Its main dining room is filled with atmosphere.

A few miles east of **Zonicle's** along the coastline with its beautiful views are the stone ruins of the **Richmond Hill-Newfield Plantation**. It is overgrown but some ruins, including slave quarters and the main house, can be seen if you wish to explore.

A few miles further east you will come across **Port Howe**, a small picuresque village known for its rich pineapple-yielding red soil and, in days gone by, its wrecking. It still boasts the ruins of the Deveaux Plantation, a large stone building which once had three storeys. The remains of this once stately manor still have some of their internal structures intact. A little of the once decorative ceiling can just be seen. It is said that French artisans were brought in to decorate the house. There is also a kitchen ruin with red stone bricks and a wooden middle beam.

The Port Howe Estate was believed to have been built by the intrepid Colonel Andrew Deveaux who recaptured Nassau from Spain in 1783. At one time, the plantation grew Georgia cotton and had barns and storage houses. Today it is mostly overgrown but the remains of the once grand and elegant plantation houses are still to be seen.

Along the coast past Port Howe there are cliffs which dip sharply into the sea and some caves. There are splendid views. Towards the east and into the heel of the boot is the easternmost point of the island, **Columbus Point**. The last couple of miles must be travelled on foot but on arrival at the point the view is worth the effort.

You will enjoy Cat Island – the rolling hills of the south, the rugged coast line and the white sand beaches of the north. The peacefulness and lack of development in many parts help to create the quietude you may be seeking.

Long Island – island of contrasts

Introduction

Long Island has been called a 'country of contrasts'. It is a long island extending about 57 miles from Cape Santa Maria to South Point and

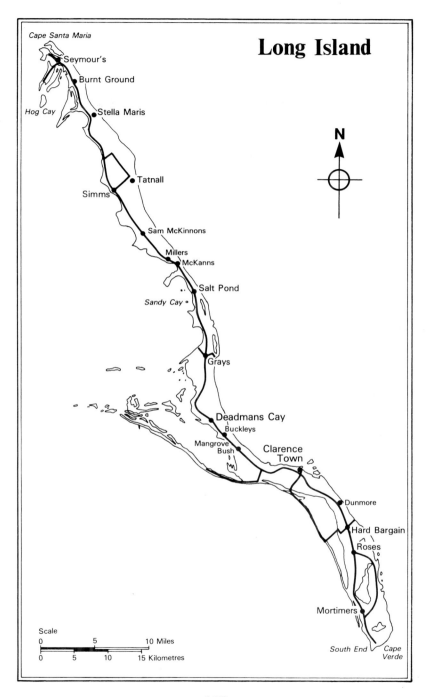

Long Island

Cape Santa Maria

Seymour's

Burnt Ground

Hog Cay

Stella Maris

N

Tatnall

Simms

Sam McKinnons

Millers

McKanns

Salt Pond

Sandy Cay

Grays

Deadmans Cay

Buckleys

Mangrove
Bush

Clarence
Town

Dunmore

Hard Bargain

Roses

Mortimers

South End   Cape
                   Verde

Scale

0   5   10 Miles

0   5   10   15 Kilometres

is nowhere wider than four miles. At its north-eastern end it has rugged cliffs plunging into the sea. On the opposite shore the area has broad white sandy beaches. In the southern part of the island lie the low, flat lands where salt used to be produced.

History

Originally called by the Arawak name Yuma, Long Island was rechristened Fernandina by Christopher Columbus on his first voyage to the New World in 1492. Archaeological evidence shows that the Lucayan Indians settled at Long Island as they did throughout the Bahamian chain of islands. After the demise of the Indians, who were carried as slaves to Hispaniola and Cuba, there was no large permanent settlement until the coming of the Loyalists. Numerous Loyalist families settled at Long Island and set up cotton plantations. They also raised cattle and sheep. Plantations flourished for only a few years. By the time of the Abolition of Slavery in 1834, most of the plantations had collapsed and been abandonded. Today there are many ruins, the majority of which are overgrown by bush, which tell of slavery days. There are also remains of some of the houses built after slavery which are usually small and built of stone. Originally they had thatched roofs; today, most are shingled. Behind the main house is a small hut with a large chimney where the cooking is done. On the older houses in Long Island, also notice fretwork on the roof tops on some of the homes throughout the island which are like crowns, birds, boats, etc. These 'signs' are supposed to keep away the evil spirits.

Long Island's population is over 5,000. It is the leading stock-rearing island and its farmers also raise corn, peas, bananas, pineapples and other crops.

Getting there

Bahamasair, the national flag-carrier, flies to **Stella Maris** about four times a week; there are more frequent flights to **Deadman's Cay**. Deadman's Cay is the largest settlement. **Carroll's Store**, where there is a good stock of grocery items and dry goods, is there. The store also serves as a pharmacy. There is also **Carroll's Guest House** which offers modest but comfortable accommodation. Deadman's Cay is near several smaller settlements including **Buckley's, Cartwright's, McKenzie** and **Mangrove Bush** which are picturesque communities where slash and burn pot-hole farming is done. One of the leading pineapple growers, Dewitt Hunt, operates in Mangrove Bush.

If you wish to explore, rent a car but drive carefully as the roads are rough in places. North of Deadman's Cay are several small settlements including **Old Gray's, Anderson's, Gray's, Bowers, Pinder's** and **Salt Pond**. The latter settlement was named for a salt pond near to its harbour anchorage on the west coast. There are several public docks with petroleum facilities and stores with marine items, groceries, meats, fresh vegetables and ice. Salt Pond is famous for being the site of the annual Long Island Regatta held in late May, which attracts many boats from throughout The Bahamas. It was inspired by the larger Family Island Regatta held in George Town each April. There is a guest house in Salt Pond owned by John McKie, an experienced sailor, and also the **Thompson Bay Inn** only a short walk away.

Preceeding north you pass a number of small settlements, usually named after families who settled there including **McKann's, Miller's, Whitehouse, Sam McKinnon's, Wemyss** and **Bain's**. After passing **Doctor's Creek** you approach **Simms**, said to be one of the oldest settlements on Long Island. Some of the descendants of the original settlers still live there today. Straw work and farming sustain the local people. Miss Ivy Simms has a small straw work factory in the settlement where she and her staff produce finely-made bags, baskets, hats and other articles. There is a lovely shaded cemetery at the Anglican Church.

The Government packing house is near to the settlement of Simms. Once a week the mail-boat calls to collect the produce brought to the packing house by the farmers of the area. The farmers sell to the Government and are thus certain of getting rid of their goods.

Beyond Simms are the settlements of **Scrub Hill, O'Neil's, Anderson** and **Millerton**. Five miles north of Millerton is **Stella Maris** which has its own airstrip, marina and hotel. It is the largest tourist development on Long Island. Founded by Johann H. Aufochs, a native of Nuremberg, the resort is still owned by Germans. The complex includes a diving centre and is well known for the **Shark Reef**. Daily excursions are taken to the 'magic' bit of reef. But there is more to Stella Maris than diving. The hotel is on a fifteen-acre

Stella Maris, Long Island (overleaf) (STELLA MARIS INN AND ESTATE)

site. It has accommodation in hotel rooms, cottages, town houses and villas. There is a restaurant plus swimming pools and a lovely beach. There is also a fine view of the island from the cliffs near the main hotel building. Ruins of the **Adderley's Plantation** can be seen but are difficult to reach unless you take a safari of machete-carrying adventurers.

About twelve miles north of Stella Maris, after passing through the villages of **Burnt Ground, Glinton** and **Seymour's** is **Cape Santa Maria** which has miles of breathtaking white sand beach. This is a good swimming spot. A small resort has been built and refurbished at Cape Santa Maria. A memorial to the Lucayanas was dedicated by Long Islanders at Cape Santa Maria, believed to be the third Bahamian landfall of Columbus.

Going South

South of Deadman's Cay and the smaller settlements immediately to the south, you will pass **Scrub Hill** and **Stevens** before arriving in **Clarence Town**. Once the largest settlement, it was formerly the capital of Long Island. It is perhaps the prettiest settlement on Long Island, some say in The Bahamas, with its most beautiful harbour and many hills. On one hill at the western end of town is **St Paul's Anglican Church**; on a hill on the eastern side is **St Peter's Catholic Church**. These large twin-towered Moorish-style churches were built by Father Jerome, the hermit of Cat Island. St Paul's was constructed before Father Jerome converted to Roman Catholicism. St Peter's was built after his conversion.

There are grocery shops in Clarence Town, a telephone station and a dock where the mail-boat calls weekly. There is also a Commissioner's Office and a clinic.

South of Clarence Town is **Dunmore**, a very small settlement which still has the plantation ruins of the old Dunmore estate. It takes determination and the help of a resident of the area to reach the ruins of a slave plantation house built of limestone with two fireplaces and chimneys. There are still drawings of sail-boats used during the plantation era on the walls. About half-a-mile from the plantation site there are two pillars, apparently the remaining gate-posts to the Dunmore Plantation.

South of Dunmore is **Hard Bargain** where Diamond Crystal had extensive salt operations. After the closure of the salt operation, World Wide Protein (Bahamas) Ltd started a shrimp farming operation. It recently closed down, however. South of Hard Bargain are **McKenzie, Taits, Roses, Berry's, Cabbage Point, Ford's, Mortimer's** and **Gordon's,** the southernmost settlement at Long Island. At Mortimer's, a local fisherman named Carlton Cartwright, while crabbing in May 1988, discovered a hidden cave and found three wooden *duhos* or ceremonial stools. These are being preserved at the Department of Archives and are held in trust until the National Museum is established.

Long Island is indeed a place which offers variety – variety of scenery, variety of accommodation and variety in architecture. It has so much that is not known; so much left to explore. Its history is rich and its scenery often breathtaking.

San Salvador – island of discovery

Introduction
Also called the land of lakes and Columbus' Isle, San Salvador is about 12 miles long and 5 miles wide. Its original name was Guanahani. Later it was called Watling's Island after George Watling, a noted buccaneer.

The cross erected to mark Columbus's landfall on San Salvador in 1492 (WENDELL CLEARE)

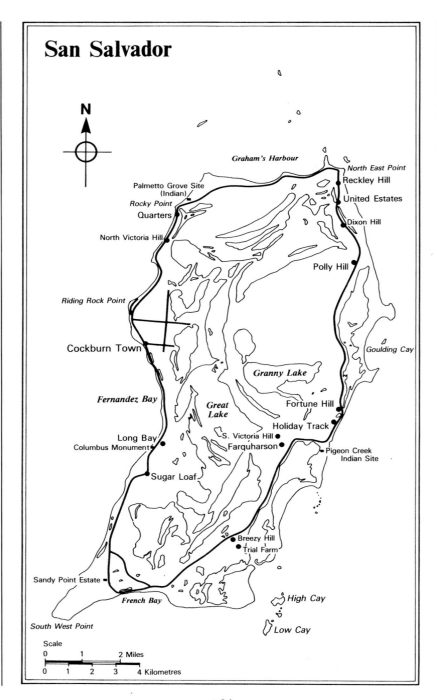

San Salvador

N

Graham's Harbour

North East Point
Reckley Hill
Palmetto Grove Site
(Indian)
Rocky Point
United Estates
Quarters
Dixon Hill
North Victoria Hill

Polly Hill

Riding Rock Point

Goulding Cay
Cockburn Town

Granny Lake

Fernandez Bay
Fortune Hill
Great
Lake
Holiday Track
Long Bay
S. Victoria Hill
Columbus Monument
Farquharson
Pigeon Creek
Indian Site
Sugar Loaf

Breezy Hill
Trial Farm

Sandy Point Estate
High Cay
French Bay
Low Cay
South West Point

Scale
0   1   2 Miles
0   1   2   3   4 Kilometres

Until recently, it was considered one of the least important of the Bahama islands. With the quincentennial celebrations in 1992, San Salvador attracted much attention as it has been for many years identified as the first landfall of Christopher Columbus in the New World. He landed at San Salvador on 12 October 1492 and was greeted by the gentle Lucayan Taino. The island has a rich history: the depopulation of its indigenous population by the Spaniards; the use of its inlets by pirates and buccaneers; the coming of the Loyalists and their slaves; the coming of the Americans during the Second World War and its aftermath; and, more recently, the advent of the tourist industry.

Throughout its history, however, most inhabitants have depended on farming. Even today, you will meet farmers on the road before or after they have visited their fields.

Getting there

The quickest way to San Salvador is by Bahamasair from Nassau which takes just over an hour. There is usually a short stop to unload and pick up passengers in Cat Island. It is also possible to travel by the mail-boat which makes a weekly stop at Cockburn Town – a longer and more leisurely trip.

Where to stay

Once in San Salvador, accommodation is available at the **Riding Rock Inn**, a first class facility with room for about 50 persons, and **Club Méditerranée Village**, built in 1992 especially for the Quincentennial celebrations in October of that year. **Ocean View** apartments at North Victoria Point are more modest in price, and very clean and comfortable. There is also the **Carter Williams' 'Motel'** which is less costly than the Riding Rock.

Seeing the island

A road, the Queen's Highway, runs round the perimeter of the island – a journey of about 35 miles. Cars can be rented from local entrepreneur Carter Williams.

You can tour the island in a day if in a desperate hurry. If you

An aerial view of the Riding Rock Inn and airstrip and the site of Club Méditerranée before construction at San Salvador (overleaf)
(BAHAMAS MINISTRY OF TOURISM)

can spare the time it is worthwhile taking two to three days to explore the various sites thoroughly.

Cockburn Town

Cockburn Town, the 'capital' of the island is possibly the best place to start a tour. It was probably named after a Governor of The Bahamas, Sir Francis Cockburn. The settlement was originally called **Riding Rocks**, named for the large boulders or rocks which at one time rolled about on the ocean floor near the settlement. The town is the centre of activity on the island. Just before reaching the main street, which is called **First Avenue**, there is the **Government complex**, which includes the clinic and nurse's residence, the Commissioner's Office, the Police Station, telegraph, Post Office and Court house. A new Roman Catholic Church, Holy Saviour, was dedicated on 12 October, 1992 to mark the Quincentennial Celebrations. Cardinal Jozef Tomko, personal envoy to Pope John Paul II, celebrated mass there on Saturday, 17 October, 1992. The

A small boutique in Cockburn Town (GAIL SAUNDERS)

San Salvador Museum, located in the ancient nineteenth century jailhouse and Commissioner's Office, includes artefacts and replicas highlighting Columbus, the Lucayans, the plantation period and nineteenth century life on San Salvador. Across from the complex is the Government dock where the mail-boat lands, bringing supplies of every kind to the island. The traditional excitement felt by the people at the arrival of the mail-boat is still apparent.

On the main road, **Queen's Highway**, just before First Avenue, is the old jail, which has hardly been used and which may become a small museum and tourist information centre. Next to the jail is the Roman Catholic Church, **Holy Saviour**, which is distinguished by a carved head of Christopher Columbus above its front door.

Turning into First Avenue, the main street of the town, on the left is the **San Salvador Public Library** which is open for a few hours almost every afternoon. Opposite is the **Ocean View Club** which has a gift shop run by the charming Ms Fernandez. There you can buy T-shirts and other souvenirs of The Bahamas. Further down the avenue is Marcus Jones' **Harlem Square Club**, where on most Friday nights a 'rip' or dance is held. Jake Jones has a food store nearly opposite. There is also the **Three Ships Restaurant and Bar** opposite the **Rip**. The restaurant serves tasty Bahamian food. There are other food stores and bars. **St Augustine's Anglican Church** is just beyond the food store. The church was consecrated in 1888 and replaced a much earlier Anglican mission.

There are small side street connecting First Avenue and the rest of Cockburn Town. It is interesting to stroll around and look at the picturesque houses and gardens. In recent times, many inhabitants have built modern cement-block houses and some boast satellite dishes which bring them into touch with the outside world.

First Avenue becomes a carriage track and continues down to Little Lake. During the nineteenth century, supplies were transported by boat from this point to the other side of the island. A new **Church of God** has recently been constructed and a **Seventh Day Adventist Church** is being built.

Leaving Cockburn Town

As you leave Cockburn Town going south, you will pass the shady almond tree at the corner of Queen's Highway and First Avenue. If you rest awhile there, you will hear the latest news and gossip.

Public cemetery

Just past the almond tree is the public cemetery, very near to the ocean. There are a few stone monuments and some broken ones bearing an anchor, a star or a cross. The earliest date is over a grave: *In Memoriam to W. Morrah Savage, Staff Commander of the Royal Navy.* He was an inspector of the imperial lighthouses and died in July 1885. His grave is the most prominent, and is surrounded by a white wooden picket fence.

Roman Catholic cemetery

Just south of the public cemetery is the **Roman Catholic cemetery** which is very small. A tall, roughly-made cross bearing the date 25 January 1891, commemorates the first Catholic mass to be held on the island since its discovery in 1492. Celebrating that mass was Father Chrysostom Scheriner, OSB who, after being saved from a shipwreck, pledged to devote his life to the Bahamian people. He died on San Salvador and was buried on the northern end of the island on the old Harbour Estate. He was largely instrumental in persuading the Government to change the island's name from Watling's Island to San Salvador.

The Heloise monument

Further south there is an overgrown path leading to the shore and to the Heloise monument which was placed there by the yawl *Heloise* while on an around-the-world cruise in 1951. It is one of the four monuments honouring the landfall of Christopher Columbus.

Long Bay Site and Columbus' monument

Continuing south you will come almost immediately to Fernandez Bay, an inlet lying between Bamboo Point and Hall Landing, an area rich in shoals and reefs for snorkelling. Just to the south is an Indian site where important contact Spanish artefacts were found by Charles Hoffman under the auspices of the College Center of the Finger Lakes, a field station of a consortium of Colleges in up-state New York, succeeded by the Bahamian Field Station. Just opposite the settlement of Long Bay is the Columbus monument, a white cross erected in December 1956 by Ruth Durlacher Wolper, an artist and writer, to commemorate Christopher Columbus' landfall. The plaque on the monument, which is widely photographed, reads: *On or near the spot Christopher Columbus landed on 12 October 1492.* This location is based on the research of Admiral S.E. Morrison. Very near to the Columbus monument stands the Mexican Olympic monument, erected in 1968 to commemorate the landfall of Columbus and the holding of the Olympic Games in the New World (i.e. Mexico) in that year. Here you can pause and have a swim in the inviting turquoise waters. During 1992, several replicas of the Spanish Caravels used by Columbus, including some from Japan and Spain, stopped at San Salvador. A re-enactment of the landfall of Columbus took place on the 500th anniversary of the landfall.

Sandy Point and Sandy Point Estate
Still travelling south, you will pass Sugar Loaf settlement on the left. On the coast is **Sugar Loaf Beach** and the **Sugar Loaf Rock** for which the entire area is named. Further south is Black Rock, an abandoned settlement. Along Sandcliff Avenue off the Queen's Highway is **Grotto Beach**, one of the loveliest beaches in The Bahamas. Further along are private homes and condominiums. Following the road along the coast you will soon come to **Sandy Point** and another breath-taking sight. Here you can just gaze at the gently rolling waves and the white sands or you may want to collect some of the many varieties of shells on this quiet and not often frequented beach.

Further east near the southern tip of the island is the **Sandy Point Estate**, also known locally as **Watling's Castle**. At this site you can see ruins of a late eighteenth century Loyalist plantation. Sandy Point is one of the many ancient plantations on San Salvador. Substantial ruins remain including the 'Great House', a kitchen and several farm buildings like barns. There are also ruins of slave quarters at the Sandy Point Estate but thick bush prevents all but the intrepid from visiting them. From the Sandy Point Estate **French Bay**, where ships once brought supplies from other settlements and islands, is visible. Sentry Tower or 'Lookout Point' was recently restored at Walting's Castle.

Belmont Church
If you follow the old Queen's Highway in an easterly direction along

The white cliffs of Graham's Harbour, San Salvador, were described by Columbus in his journal (overleaf) (GAIL SAUNDERS)

French Bay, you will see the ruins of an old Anglican Church, **St Michael's**. It is known as Belmont Church and existed in the early part of this century to serve settlements close by including Bell Mount as the area is known.

Continuing in a north-easterly direction along the old Queen's Highway, you pass **Trial Farm** and **Snow Bay Beach**. This area is very calm, good for swimming, shelling and canoeing.

Pigeon Creek

The bay goes into the mouth of **Pigeon Creek** from which there is an excellent view of High Cay, which may have been the first land sighted by Christopher Columbus on 12 October 1492. Paddling a canoe up the creek is a soothing experience. The calm is occasionally disturbed by the cries of various birds such as seagulls. In the nineteenth century, during the height of the plantation era, cattle and supplies were shipped down the creek from the Farquharson Plantation around to French Bay and often to the Sandy Point Estate.

Farquharson's Plantation

Continuing northwards along the main highway, about five miles from Belmont Church, you come to the **Farquharson Plantation** which is not far from the Pigeon Creek School. The plantation is on the left side of the road and has a quarry just beneath it. Follow the path up the hill and you will soon come to quite a number of ruins including the 'Great House' and the kitchen, which has a fireplace and brick oven. There are ruins of several estate buildings north of the Great House and slave quarters can be found some distance to the south.

Charles Farquharson, who was Justice of the Peace for Watling's Island, kept a journal for 1831 to 1832. It has been published as *A Relic of Slavery* and from it we learn of the workings of the estate. Its chief crop was guinea corn which was chiefly a subsistence crop, grown as food for slaves. Some surplus was shipped to Nassau. There were other crops such as pigeon peas, sweet potatoes, cabbage and pumpkins. There was also some stock on the estate and mules and horses were used for transport. The sea yielded salt and fish. In 1832 there were 56 slaves on the plantation.

Pigeon Creek Indian site

Continuing northward along the main road for just over a mile, you will reach the **Pigeon Creek Indian site**. Archaeological excavations, conducted mainly by the College Center for the Finger Lakes' archaeologists, have shown that the peaceful Arawak-Taino people, the indigenous people of The Bahamas, had villages there. These Lucayans, as they are also called, met Christopher Columbus when he first set foot on San Salvador on 12 October 1492. Unfortunately, the Spaniards carried them away to work in the gold and silver mines of Hispaniola and Cuba. No descendant of these people live in The Bahamas today; there are some pottery objects, shells and other artefacts still in existence – the remains of the Arawak culture.

Just south of the Pigeon Creek site is **The Bluff** which can be explored by the energetic visitor. The hike along the bluff is about one and a half miles and leads to a fantastic sandy beach – Snow Bay Beach.

Dixon Hill

Leaving the Pigeon Creek site and continuing northwards along the main road will bring you to **Fortune Hill** and **Polly Hill** on the left, the sites of two nineteenth century plantations. On the left are Storr's Lake and East Beach. By following a path from the beach, you can get to Crab Cay where another monument to mark Christopher Columbus' discovery of the New World was placed by 1891 by the *Chicago Herald* newspaper. Just before **United Estates**, the largest settlement on the island, is **Dixon Hill**, the site of the Dixon Hill Lighthouse built by the Imperial Lighthouse Service in 1887 and renovated in 1930. Standing 163 feet above sea-level, the lighthouse has 400,000 candle power and a visibility of 19 miles. It flashes every ten seconds. The lighthouse is named after John Dixon, the stepson of Charles Farquharson. From the lighthouse there is a breath-taking view of the island. To the east is the ocean and to the west the inland lake system.

The northern end of the island

Further north is **Reckley Hill** which was originally settled by the Pratt family. The buildings of the former United States Coastguard Station at Northeast Point can still be seen. It is now the site of the Government Secondary School. The station beamed navigational signals which were used by ships and airplanes. Around Rice Bay and past North Point is the **Bahamian Field Station**, a Bahamian

The nineteenth century lighthouse on Dixon Hill (GAIL SAUNDERS)

Limited, non-profit-making company. The Bahamian Field Station is a field station which specialises in geology and archaeology. Its director is Dr Donald T. Gerace. From the field station there is a view of North Point and Cut Cay, which was mentioned by

Christopher Columbus in his *Journal*. Continuing westward along the main road which hugs the coast you pass Harbour Yard, a part of the Harbour Estate. The plantation was owned by the Loyalist Burton Williams. Near the road you will see a cross which marks the grave of the Roman Catholic Priest, Father Chrysostom Schreiner OSB, who started a mission on San Salvador in 1925. Apparently, Burton Williams is buried under Chrysostom's grave. There are a few ruins of the old **Harbour Estate** and also remains of the RAF Hotel which was used during the Second World War. The Columbus Hotel, as it was called, was built in the 1930s by Sir Harry Oakes who leased it to the RAF during the War.

The New World Museum
Further south on the Queen's Highway are **Polaris Point** and the **New World Museum**, founded in 1958 by Ruth Durlacher Wolper, an American. The Museum houses Lucayan pottery, paintings of Columbus' landfall, a petroglyph (rock carving) from a cave in Rum Cay, mortars and pestles, and shell artefacts from Lucayan times. There is a small admission fee; drinks can be purchased from a small bar at the back. It is relaxing to sit and sip a cool drink on the beach front beneath the shady coconut trees.

Riding Rock Point
On the way south you will pass North Victoria Hill, a small settlement. There is a magnificent beach on the right. Before Riding Rock Point is Bonefish Bay, renowned for its fine bonefish and excellent for swimming. **Club Mediterranée** recently opened a holiday village adjacent to a beautiful beach. Several years ago the site, which was originally built by the Pan American Corporation to track civilian missiles, was used by the Central Secondary School and before that by the campus of the San Salvador Teacher's Training College which has since become a part of the College of The Bahamas. Nearly adjacent to Club Mediterranée is the airport.

A tour of the island leaves the visitor with a sense of the past and a feeling of peace. San Salvador is an island not only of history but also of beauty and tranquillity.

Rum Cay
Twenty miles south-west of San Salvador is Rum Cay, a small,

sparsely populated island. It has a resort – the **Rum Cay Dive Club** which has 14 rooms and is owned by David Melville, who employs most of the Rum Cay residents. Before visiting Rum Cay, check to see whether the Club is open.

Rum Cay is mainly flat but has a few rolling hills rising to about 120 feet. The island was named Santa Maria de la Concepcion by Columbus. The modern name Rum Cay is said to be in memory of a wreck destroyed with a cargo of rum which foundered off the coral reefs which abound around the island's shore.

Farming has been the mainstay of the island's economy. Salt was also once raked and cattle reared.

The main settlement is **Port Nelson**. It is a picturesque village lying among coconut groves. There is a local bar and restaurant run by the Bains and another restaurant operated by Delores Wilson.

There is a 2,500-foot airstrip west of Port Nelson which accommodates charter flights and private planes. The **Rum Cay Club** is popular with divers, snorkellers and beachcombers. There are other watersports available.

For divers there is the wreck of the 101-gun Man-of-War HMS *Conqueror*, which was built in Devon in 1855 and served in the Crimean War. It sank near Rum Cay in 1861 and is located in 30 feet of water. Known as the 'underwater museum of The Bahamas', it is the property of The Bahamas Government and none of the contents of the ship may be removed.

The Islands to the South

Crooked Island, Acklins and Long Cay

Those who wish to get completely off the beaten track should travel to the southern islands in The Bahamas. These are not really tourist islands but have natural beauty and some amenities. A new administration complex was recently opened in Colonel Hill. It houses the Commissioner's Office, Post Office, Courtroom, Police Station and jail. A clinic was recently opened at Landrail Point and an **Old Folk's Home** at Moss Town. There is also a park at Colonel Hill.

Crooked Island and **Acklins** are enclosed in a shallow lagoon known as the Bight of Acklins. The islands were not permanently settled until the coming of the Loyalists in the late 1780s. Very soon after their arrival they set up over forty cotton plantations employing over a thousand slaves. As elsewhere in The Bahamas, infertile soil and the chenille bug destroyed the crops, and the plantations quickly declined. Many proprietors left the islands and sold some of the slaves to proprietors in the sugar islands further south.

Today, the islands are sparsely populated. They offer tranquillity and some ruins of ages long past. Included among these ruins is the building said to be the first Post Office in The Bahamas which is located at **Pitt's Town**. This ruin probably sits near the spot where the monthly packet-boat landed on its way through the **Crooked Island Passage** from Jamaica to Britain. It was at Pitt's Town that it dropped mail and passengers, many of whom went on to Nassau or other islands in The Bahamas. Close to Pitt's Town and the **Bird Rock Lighthouse** is **Marine Farm Plantation**, which, like **Hope Guest House**, was left by the late Herbert McKinney of Nassau to The Bahamas National Trust. Marine Farm, located near to the north-western tip of Crooked Island, overlooks the Crooked Island Passage – a magnificent view. It has ancient British fortifications, some of which can still be seen. It is believed that Christopher Columbus landed near this area in 1492 on his voyage through The Bahamas.

South of Pitt's Town is **Landrail Point**, a good anchorage described by the *Yachtsman's Guide 1987* as a 'pretty settlement' with many citrus trees. There is a quaint restaurant, store and guesthouse run by Marina Gibson where delicious meals are served. **Hope House**, an ancient plantation ruin, can be reached on foot.

From Pitt's Town, further east along the northern coast of Crooked Island, is **Colonel Hill**. The 3500-foot airstrip is near this settlement and contact should be made with the Bahamasair agent if you wish to reserve accommodation. There are weekly flights to this island. There is the **Crooked Island Beach Inn** near Colonel Hill and also the **T and S Guest House** at Colonel Hill. The Commissioner's Office is located at this settlement, from which there is a magnificent view of all of Crooked Island. Eunice Deleveaux has a store and Julius Bonaby operates a tavern a short distance away. There is a telephone service.

Acklins

Acklins Island forms the eastern side of the Crooked Island triangle. There are many bays and caves along the coast. Settlements have inviting names such as **Delectable Bay, Lovely Bay, Snug**

179

Corner, **Golden Grove** and **Spring Point**. These are joined by
a road which connects the settlements from Lovely Bay to Morant
Bay in the south. Acklins, like Crooked Island, once had cotton
plantations but these soon declined. Today Acklin islanders are
mainly farmers.

Hard Hill, with ruins of a lookout tower, is the highest point.
At the southern end of the island of Acklins is **Castle Island** which
has a lighthouse. It must be approached by boat.

Long Cay

On the south-western side of Crooked Island is Long Cay, once
known as Fortune Island. Its main settlement, **Albert Town**, is now
very sparsely populated though it was once a prosperous little town.
It was engaged in the sponge and salt industries and also served as
a port from which stevedores were engaged to serve on the German,
American and Dutch boats which then travelled to South America
and the Caribbean. There are good fishing grounds around the
waters of Long Cay.

Mayaguana

Mayaguana, which still retains its Arawak name, is sparsely populated with farmers and fishermen, and is not visited by many tourists.
Its largest settlement, **Abraham's Bay** (which is near the airstrip)
houses the Commissioner's Office and a telephone station. It also
has several stores and a small restaurant and guest-house. There are
two other substantial settlements, **Betsy Bay** on the coast in the
east and **Pirate's Well** in the north. It is possible to anchor off this
settlement, although it may be choppy at times. The people of
Mayaguana are very friendly.

Inagua – the salt island and flamingo country

Inagua is the most southerly and third largest island in The Bahamas.
Its name is a corruption of its earlier designation, Heneagua, derived
from a Spanish word meaning 'water is to be found there'. Although
it is mostly low and flat, it has James Hill on the north coast rising
to 90 feet, East Hill rising to 132 feet and Salt Pond Hill on the south
coast rising to 102 feet. There is no natural harbour and most of
its coast is fringed by a reef.

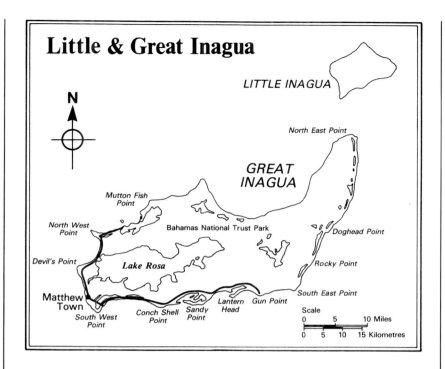

Little & Great Inagua

LITTLE INAGUA

N

North East Point

GREAT
INAGUA

Mutton Fish
Point

North West
Point

Bahamas National Trust Park

Doghead Point

Devil's Point

Lake Rosa

Rocky Point

South East Point

Matthew
Town

Lantern   Gun Point
Head

South West
Point

Conch Shell
Point

Sandy
Point

Scale

0   5   10 Miles

0   5   10   15 Kilometres

History

Permanently settled in the middle of the nineteenth century, Inagua, because of its low rainfall and tradewinds, has natural salt ponds. After the separation of Turks Island from The Bahamas in 1848, a joint-stock company, the Heneagua Salt Pond Company, was formed to cultivate the salt ponds on the island. Another company, the Inagua Tramway and Salt Company, was established by a group of Nassau businessmen in 1865. With the decline of the salt industry after 1870 because of the inability to find new salt markets, the economy was sustained by the stevedoring business. Many American, German and Dutch boats stopped at **Matthew Town** to collect willing Bahamian labourers who were used to load and unload cargoes at West Indian and South American ports. This business was dealt a blow by the outbreak of the First World War which interrupted shipping.

Salt and stevedoring were revived on a small scale by A.L. Symonette during the early 1930s. It was a New Englander, J.M. Erickson, and his two brothers who revived the salt industry on a large scale in the late 1930s near Lake Rosa. The Ericksons greatly expanded salt production using manual as well as mechanised methods. Later in the 1950s, the Ericksons sold out to the Morton Salt Company which further modernised the salt industry. Today about a million tonnes of salt are harvested annually by the company. About 12,000 acres have been set aside for salt production. Arrangements can be made with the Morton Salt Company to see its salt ponds and also the loading docks in Man-o'-War Bay.

Matthew Town

Matthew Town, named for Governor George Matthew (Governor of The Bahamas 1844 – 1849), was laid out during his tenure and is the chief settlement in Inagua. It is said to be the best laid out town in The Bahamas. It has an airstrip from which Bahamasair flies weekly to Nassau. The Commissioner's Office is there and it has a telephone and clinic. The mail-boat also calls weekly. It is a port of entry and has well-stocked grocery stores and a hardware store.

Visitor accommodation is limited. **The Morton Salt Company** operates a small, basic guest house and serves Bahamian food. There is also **Ford's Guest House**. Bookings should be made in advance before leaving Nassau. A modern state-of-the-art telecommunications system was recently installed at Matthew Town. Residents and visitors can call or fax anywhere in the world.

Wildlife

Inagua is of interest to sportsmen and naturalists. It has a large savannah or prairie in the centre where wild cattle, donkeys and boar are said to roam. There is also a large shallow lake, formerly Lake Windsor, now known as Lake Rosa, which is about 12 miles long. Near the upper part of the lake is the flamingo-breeding ground.

Flamingoes, which are native to The Bahamas, were first described in the 1740s by Mark Catesby, a famous naturalist. At that time, and for many years after, the flamingo inhabited other parts of the Bahamian archipelago. Lake Rosa in the centre of Inagua was the flamingo's last stronghold. In the 1950s, the 'Society for the Protection of the Flamingo in The Bahamas', the predecessor of The Bahamas National Trust, was formed. It persuaded the Government to declare the bird a protected species. Today, under The Bahamas National Trust, the flamingo reserve has become the **Inagua National Park** and covers an area of 287 square miles. It is the home

The Bahama parrot (THE BAHAMAS NATIONAL TRUST)

of the largest colony of West Indian flamingoes in the Caribbean.
As well as the beautiful flamingo, with its various shades of pink,
its elegant neck and distinctive long legs, there are many other birds,

such as Bahamian parrots, West Indian tree ducks, humming-birds, roseate spoonbills, pelicans, blue herons and the rare reddish egret. Inagua is a haven for bird-watchers and nature-lovers who can make arrangements to stay at The Bahamas National Trust camp about 23 miles from Matthew Town. (Write to the Bahamas National Trust, P.O. Box N4105, Nassau, Bahamas.) The two wardens, James Nixon and Theo Moss, will arrange a jeep tour to see some really wonderful sites. A round trip from Matthew Town will take about a day.

| 9 |
Night-life

For those who wish to enjoy the swinging night-life of Nassau and Paradise Island there are many bars, night-clubs, discos and casinos to choose from.

Gambling at the Paradise Island Casino (RESORTS INTERNATIONAL)

Casinos

In Nassau there are two casinos – the plush and recently refurbished **Paradise Island Resort and Casino** and the newer **Cable Beach Casino.**

The Paradise Island Casino is said to be the largest in The Bahamas and indeed the Caribbean. Like the Cable Beach Casino it offers blackjack, craps, roulette, baccarat and hundreds of croupiers working with tables. Within each complex there are dining areas with entertainment of the highest quality. Both casinos have theatres.

Le Cabaret Theatre attached to Paradise Island Casino features a Las Vegas-style spectacular show providing comedy, glitter and glamour. At Le Cabaret you can have dinner or cocktails and watch the show. Other entertainment includes disco music at **Club Pastiche** and a leading Bahamian band at **Tradewinds.** There are over ten restaurants nearby where you can dine. **The Cable Beach Casino** also has dining areas very near. These include **The Regency Room, The Riviera, Pirate's Inn** and **King Conch Cafe.** The **Bahamas Rhythm Theatre** attached to the Cable Beach Casino offers a lavish Broadway-style musical nightly. Both shows feature dancers, singers and all sorts of surprises.

In Freeport, visit **Princess Casino** (formerly called El Casino).

The Drumbeat Club on West Bay Street (G. W. LENNOX)

This is located in a lavish Moorish-style building and has hundreds of slot machines plus roulette wheels and blackjack tables. Attached to this is the **Casino Royale Theatre** which offers a French-style lido show featuring dancers, singers and comedians.

The newly renovated hotel in Freeport, the Lucayan Beach Hotel, also has a casino – perhaps not as plush as Princess Casino but still offering great challenges and fun to visitors.

Night-clubs

For those who wish to see something more typically Bahamian, a visit to Peanuts Taylor's **Drumbeat Club** on West Bay Street in Nassau is recommended. There are two shows nightly, at 8.30 p.m. and 10.30 p.m. There you can feel the real soul of the Bahamian as you listen to Peanuts on the goombay drums, and witness the fire dance and limbo. There is also a lively band to dance to. It is possible to have dinner at this club.

Disco music

For disco music in Nassau try **Club Mystique** at the Cable Beach Inn, **El Galleon II** which is located on a 93-foot eighteenth century Spanish galleon replica, **Confetti's** on Bay and Deveaux Streets, a new first-class night spot, **The Palace** on Elizabeth Avenue, the **Out Island Bar** in the Nassau Beach Hotel and the **Junkanoo Lounge** in the Cable Beach Hotel.

Dancing

Dancing is also offered at the **Buccaneer Lounge**, Loew's Harbour Cove Hotel, Paradise Island, **Candy's**, Poinciana Inn, Bernard Road, **Disco Altitude**, Paradise Island, **Disco 2001**, Blue Hill Road, **Family Island Lounge**, Soldier Road, **Keyboard Lounge**, Marlborough Street, **Le Paon**, the Grand Hotel, **The Palm Court Bar**, Ambassador Beach Hotel, Cable Beach, **Patio Bar** and **Sand Bar**, Ambassador Beach Hotel, **Pirate's Tavern Restaurant and Bar**, Bay and East Streets, **Rendezvous Lounge**, Paradise Island, **Super Disco Enterprises**, Kensington Gardens, downtown Nassau and **Valentine's Love Club**, Bay and Nassau Streets, Nassau.

Dancing in Freeport

Native shows and dancing are offered at the **Bahamia Club** in The Bahamas Princess Hotel and the **Yellow Bird Show Club**, which is in close proximity to the International Bazaar. There are also several discos which attract large crowds. These include the **Panache** nightclub, located in the Holiday Inn in Lucaya, the **Sultan's Tent Disco** in the Princess Towers Hotel and **Studio 69** at Lucayan Bay.

On the Family Islands there are fewer clubs but in each large settlement in many of the islands there is a club with music. Usually local bands play at weekends. The best way to find out about the night-life on the islands is by asking at the hotel or guest-house when you arrive. You may be lucky and be there at a time when superb local bands, some of which have performed in the USA, are performing. Then the usually quiet atmosphere of these places really livens up.

Theatre

Serious drama, musicals, an occasional opera and the finest entertainment can be experienced at the **Dundas Centre for the Performing Arts**. The repertory season runs from January through May. For details of Dundas shows call 393-3728. Shows usually begin at 8.30 p.m. and tickets are usually modest in price.

After the repertory season there are various plays and shows put on at the Dundas by local dramatic groups including the Nassau Amateur Operatic Society, the Nassau Players, the University Players and James Catlyn and Friends. These groups provide a variety of entertainment ranging from locally written plays and skits to Gilbert and Sullivan operas. Ring the Dundas number for information.

| 10 |
Useful information about The Bahamas

Climate

The Bahamas has been called 'the isles of June'. A temperate climate prevails and there are few sudden changes in temperature. The Bahamian winter, which runs from December to April, has temperatures ranging from 70° – 80°F (21° – 26°C). Winter temperatures rarely fall below 60°F and in the summer the thermometer rarely rises above 90°F. Although the humidity is high, the sea breezes, the North East Trades, compensate for the summer heat. The islands have very bright sunlight; the sun shines almost every day. Rainfall averages about 50 inches a year.

The Bahamas' hurricane season runs from June until November, but August, September and October are the high-risk months. The Bahamas has escaped being hit by a bad hurricane for many years.

Clothing

Lighweight, casual clothing is what tourists will mostly need in The Bahamas. For dining at the better restaurants men will need a jacket and tie and women a cocktail dress or dressy pants-suit. During the winter season tourists may want to dress up to attend special events.

Beach wear should include a long-sleeved blouse or cover-up to protect the skin from the sun during the extremely sunny morning and early afternoon hours. In the winter a sweater may come in handy and it is always wise to carry a fold-up umbrella.

'Duty Free' shopping

'Duty Free' shopping is available in The Bahamas. Now available at bargain prices are cameras and camera equipment, jewellery, leather goods, liquors, perfumes and colognes, table linens and crocheted linens, watches and clocks.

Currency

The Bahamian dollar is held on par with the US dollar and both currencies can be spent throughout the Commonwealth. Bahamian paper money runs in half dollar, $1, $3, $5, $10, $20, $50 and $100 bills. Coins come in 1, 5, 10, 15, 25 and 50 cent pieces.

Banks handle currency exchanges in The Bahamas during regular banking hours, that is from 9:30 a.m. to 3 p.m. Monday through Thursday and 9:30 a.m. to 5 p.m. on Friday. Some hotels change small amounts of foreign currency. Expect to pay a small commission on exchange of travellers' cheques.

On the Family Islands most banks, if there is a branch, are only open a few days a week and then only for a few hours. You should change your money before you arrive on the more remote Family Islands. In the large hotels and better restaurants in Nassau and Freeport major credit cards are usually accepted.

Tipping
The usual rate of tipping is 15 per cent. Many hotels and restaurants include the gratuity in the bill.

Postal services
Nassau and Freeport Post Offices are opened from 8:30 a.m. to 5:30 p.m. Monday to Friday and from 8:30 a.m. to 12:30 p.m. on

The 'Harley and Charley' mailboat at Governor's Harbour, Eleuthera (GAIL SAUNDERS)

Saturdays. On the Family Islands, Post Offices may be opened only for a few days a week. Air letters to all destinations are 40 cents. Airmail to the USA, the West Indies and Canada are 45 cents per half ounce. The rate is 50 cents per half ounce to the United Kingdom, Central and South America, Bermuda, Falkland and the islands of the Mediterranean and Europe.

All countries in Africa, Asia, Australia, New Zealand and the islands of the Pacific and Indian Oceans are 60 cents per half ounce.

Telecommunications

The telephone system in The Bahamas is run by a Government Corporation, Bahamas Telecommunications Corporation or BATELCO. Direct dialling is available to many of the islands from North America, Europe, the United Kingdom and Japan. The Bahamas' area code is 809. Direct dialling from Nassau and Freeport and some of the Family Islands is available. An operator-assisted call is however necessary on many of the Family Islands.

Driving in The Bahamas

The British custom of driving on the left is still practised in The Bahamas. Most cars in The Bahamas have the steering wheel on the left side so be careful when overtaking. Speed limits within city limits are usually 25 mph. On roads in New Providence just outside the city the speed limit is 30 mph. On a few highways in Nassau and Freeport you may travel at 45 mph. There are traffic lights in Nassau and Freeport. Marsh Harbour, Abaco, and Governor's Harbour, Eleuthera have the only traffic lights in the Family Islands.

Car and motor-scooter rentals

Cars and motor-scooters can be rented in Nassau, Grand Bahama and on the major Family Islands. A valid driver's licence is accepted for up to three months. Credit cards are usually needed to rent cars and motor-scooters. Crash helmets, which are supplied by the rental agency, are compulsory for scooter drivers and passengers.

Electric current

The Bahamas has standard North American current, 110 volts, 60 cycles. European travellers or those with 220 volt appliances should bring adaptors.

Embassies and Consulates

The Bahamas maintains diplomatic relations with many countries. Many of the representatives are honorary. The offices maintained in The Bahamas by foreign governments include:

BRITISH HIGH COMMISSION, Bitco Building, 3rd floor, East Street, P.O. Box N7516, Nassau, Tel: 325-7471/4.

UNITED STATES EMBASSY, Mosmar Building, Queen Street, P.O. Box N8197, Tel: 322-1181, 322-4753, and 322-1700.

EMBASSY OF THE REPUBLIC OF HAITI, Nassau, P.O. Box N666, Nassau. Tel: 322-2109.

Holidays

Below are days when public holidays are observed in The Bahamas. Businesses close on these days.

New Year's Day (1 January)
Good Friday
Easter Monday
Whit Monday (seven weeks after Easter)
Labour Day (first Friday in June)
Independence Day (10 July)
Emancipation Day (first Monday in August)
Discovery Day (12 October)
Christmas Day (25 December)
Boxing Day (26 December)

Those holidays falling on a Saturday or Sunday are usually observed on the following Monday.

Medical facilities

The major hotels in Nassau and Freeport have a doctor on call. In Nassau there is a large, well-equipped Government-operated hospital, the **Princess Margaret Hospital**, and in Freeport there is the **Rand Memorial Hospital**. In Nassau there is a private hospital, **Doctor's Hospital**, on Shirley Street and Collins Avenue. On the major Family Islands there are resident doctors or nurses and clinics. In cases of emergency planes can be booked to take patients into Nassau or in some cases into the United States.

Cruise ships in Nassau Harbour (LISA ADDERLEY)

Hospitals

Princess Margaret Hospital, Shirley Street, Nassau, Tel. 322-2861.

Doctor's Hospital, Shirley Street and Collins Avenue, Nassau, Tel. 322-8411 or 322-8414.

Rand Memorial Hospital, East Atlantic Drive, Freeport, Tel. 352-6735.

Religion

Bahamians are a very religious people. Churches abound. Denominations include: Anglican, Baptist, Christian Science, Church of God, Hebrew Congregation, Jehovah's Witness, Lutheran, Methodist, Plymouth Brethren, Presbyterian, Roman Catholic, Seventh Day Adventist and Islam.

Shopping hours

Shops usually open at 9 a.m. or 9.30 a.m. and close between 5 p.m. and 6 p.m. Some shops have different hours of opening on Thursday, Friday and Saturday.

Tourist information

The Bahamas attracts over three million visitors to its shores every year. In order to assist visitors and organise tourist amenities there is a Ministry of Tourism. Its headquarters is located in Nassau at the Market Plaza on Bay Street. Information of all types can be had from this office. The telephone numbers are 322-7500/4.

In addition, there are information booths at:
Nassau International Airport, tel: 325-9251 or 325-9297.
Prince George Wharf, tel: 325-9155.
Rawson Square, Bay Street, tel: 325-9171.
Nassau/Paradise Island Promotion Board, Hotel House, West Bay St., tel: 322-8381/2/3/4.

In Freeport information booths are located at:
Freeport International Airport
Freeport Harbour Cruiseship Port
International Bazaar, West Sunrise Highway, tel: 352-8044.
Grand Bahama Promotion Board, Sir Charles Hayward Library, East Mall, Freeport, tel: 352-7845, 352-8356.

The Bahamas has numerous tourist offices in the United States.

The Bahamas Tourist offices

Atlanta, 2957 Clairmont Road, Suite 150, Atlanta, Georgia 30345, Tel. (404) 633-1793.
Boston, 1027 Statler Office Building, Boston, Mass. 02116, Tel. (617) 426-3144.
Charlotte, 1000 Independence Tower, 4801 E Independence Boulevard, Charlotte, North Carolina, 28212, Tel. (704) 532-1290.
Chicago, 8600 W. Bryn Mawr Avenue, Suite 820, Chicago, Illinois, 60631. Tel. (312) 693-1111.
Dallas, World Trade Center, POB 581408, Dallas, Texas, 75258, Tel. (214) 742-1886.
Detroit, 26400 Lasher Road, Southfield, Mich. 48034, Tel. (313) 357-2940.
Frankfurt am Main, Moerfelder Landstrasse 45-47, D-6000 Frankfurt/Main 70, Germany, Tel. 69 62 6051 Fax: 69 62 7311.
Houston, 5177 Richmond Ave., Suite 755, Houston, Tx. 77056, Tel. (713) 626-1566.

London, Bahamas House, 10 Chesterfield St., London, England, W1X-8AH, Tel. 071-629-5238.

Los Angeles, 3450 Wilshire Boulevard, Los Angeles, Calif.90014. Tel. (213) 385-0033.

Miami, 255 Alhambra Circle, Coral Gables. Fla. 33134, Tel. (305) 442-4860.

Milan, Foro Buonaparte 68, 20121 Milano, Italy, Tel. 02/72023003-2526 Fax: 72023123.

Montreal, 1255 Phillips Square, Montreal, Quebec, H3B3G1, Tel. (514) 861-6797.

New York, 150 E. 52nd Street, New York, N.Y. 10022, Tel. (212) 758-2777.

Paris, 7 Boulevard de la Madeleine, 75001 Paris, France, Tel. 42-61-60-20 or 42-61-61-30.

Philadelphia, 437 Chestnut Street, Philadelphia, PA. 19102, Tel. (215) 925-0876.

San Francisco, 44 Montgomery Street, Suite 500, San Francisco, California 94104, Tel. (415) 398-5502.

Tokyo, 4-9-17 Akasaka, Minato-ku, Tokyo, 107, Japan, Tel. (813) 470-6162.

Toronto, 121 Bloor Street East, Suite 1101, Toronto, Ontaria, M4W 3M5, Tel. (416) 968-2999.

Vancouver, 470 Granville Street, Vancouver, B.C. V6C1V5, Tel. (604) 688-8334.

Washington, D.C., 1730 Rhode Island Ave., N.W., Washington, D.C. 20036, Tel. (202) 659-9135.

Travel formalities

Immigration

Citizens of the United States do not need a passport or visa to enter The Bahamas if their stay is limited to eight months or less. Identification needed is a birth certificate, voter's registration card or driver's licence with a photograph. United Kingdom and Canadian visitors do not need a passport or visa unless they are staying over three weeks. Citizens from other countries need a passport. Check with the nearest British Embassy to see if a visa is needed.

A departure tax of $13 is charged on leaving the airport.

Customs

You must clear immigration and customs at an official port of entry whether you travel by private plane, boat or a commercial airline.

Each person must declare his/her belongings and bags may be inspected.

Visitors may bring in personal belongings, a quart of liquor, 50 cigars or 200 cigarettes, one quart of wine and small gifts worth $100 or less.

It is prohibited to bring in firearms unless you have a Bahamian gun licence, animals unless you have a permit from the Ministry of Agriculture and Fisheries, and marijuana or narcotics of any kind. Drug trafficking is a serious offence and the smallest amount of it found will lead to your arrest.

US Customs allow their citizens to take home duty free $400 worth of articles provided that they have been away from the United States for 48 hours. There are limitations on the amount of cigars, cigarettes, liquors and perfume which can be included in this exemption.

Transportation

Taxis

Taxi rates are usually about $2 for the first quarter of a mile. Each additional quarter mile costs about 30 cents. The fare between Nassau's International Airport and Cable Beach is about $10; to downtown Nassau, about $14; to Paradise Island, roughly about $20. In Freeport a ride from the airport to downtown Freeport costs about $8. Prices are always rising.

On the Family Islands, taxi fares vary. You should always ask how much the fare is before taking the ride.

Bus and jitney service

Jitneys or small buses service visitors and residents in New Providence. Fares range from 75 cents to $1. In Freeport, there is a red double-decker bus which stops at the major hotels and sight-seeing attractions. There is also a bus service on Paradise Island.

Car rentals

Major international rental companies such as Hertz, Avis, National

Jitney buses at their stand in Nassau, waiting to take passengers to the western areas of the island (MICHAEL BOURNE)

and others service Nassau, Freeport and Paradise Island. Usually, on the Family Islands, individuals rent cars. Some hotels also rent cars to their guests. If you drive remember to keep to the left!

Further reading

General

Albury, Paul   *The Story of The Bahamas* (London, 1975).

Cash, P., Gordon, S., and Saunders, G.   *Sources of Bahamian History* (London 1991).

Collingwood, Dean and Dodge, Steve   *Modern Bahamian Society* (Parkersburg, Iowa, 1989).

Craton, Michael   *A History of The Bahamas* (London, 1962, revised 1968). Reprinted 1986.

Moseley, M.   *Bahamas Handbook* (Nassau, 1926).

Saunders, Hartley   *The Other Bahamas* (Nassau, 1991).

Stark, J.H.   *History of and Guide to the Bahamas Islands* (Boston, 1891).

Stevenson   *The Bahamas Reference Annual 1985* (Nassau, 1985).

Insight Guides, Bahamas (APA Productions, Malaysia, 1986).

Family islands

Barratt, P.J.H.   *Grand Bahama* (Harrisburg, 1972).

Dodge, Steve   *Abaco: The History of an Out Island and is Cays* (Miami, Tropic Isle, 1983).

Durrell, Z.C.   *The Innocent Island: Abaco in the Bahamas* (Vermont, 1972).

Erickson, M.O.   *Great Inagua* (New York 1987).

Klingel, G.C.   *Inagua* (London, 1944).

Young, E.   *Eleuthera, The Island Called Freedom* (London, 1966).

Loyalists

Parrish, Lydia A.   Records of some Southern Loyalists. Collected from 1940 – 1953 (Typed manuscript in Widener Library, Harvard University).

Peters, Thelma P.   The American Loyalists and the Plantation Period in the Bahama Islands (Ph.D. Thesis, University of Florida, 1960).

Sunset on Saunders Beach (MICHAEL BOURNE)

Riley, Sandra *Homeward Bound. A History of the Bahama Islands to 1850* (Miami, 1983).

Saunders, Gail *Bahamian Loyalists and Their Slaves* (London, 1983).

Slavery

Peggs, A.D. (ed.) *A Relic of Slavery. Farquharson's Journal, 1831 – 1832* (Nassau, 1957).

Public Records Office, Nassau *Aspects of Slavery* (Nassau, 1973).

Public Records Office, Nassau *Aspects of Slavery II* (Nassau, 1984).

Saunders, Gail *Slavery in The Bahamas, 1638 – 1838* (Nassau, 1985).

Shattuck, G.B. (ed.) *The Bahamas Islands* (New York and London, 1905) see J.M. Wright's chapter on History of the Bahamas. It was also published separately as *History of the Bahamas* (Baltimore, 1908).

Religion

Canzoneri, A. and Symonette, M. *Baptists in the Bahamas. A Historical Review* (El Paso, 1977).

Coleman, J.B. *Upon these Rocks. Catholics in the Bahamas* (St John's Abbey Press, Minnesota, 1973).

Education

Bain, R.E. Education Policy in the Bahamas up to 1823 and its determinants (M.A. Thesis, London University, 1959).

Bethel, Keva M. Perceived Effectiveness of Teacher Education Programs in The Bahamas (Ph.D. Edmonton, University of Albert, 1981).

Trainor, J. A Study of Formal Education in the Bahamas (Ph.D. Thesis, Syracuse University, 1982).

Williams, Colbert *The Methodist Contribution to Education in The Bahamas* (Gloucester, 1982).

Prohibition

Cash, Philip Colonial Policies and Outside Influences. A Study of Bahamian History (M.A. Thesis, University of Wales, 1979).

Industries

Public Records Office, Nassau *The Sponging Industry* (Nassau, 1974).

Public Records Office, Nassau   *The Pineapple Industry* (Nassau, 1977).

Public Records Office, Nassau   *The Salt Industry in the Bahamas* (Nassau, 1980).

Public Records Office, Nassau   *The Boat-Building Industry in the Bahamas* (Nassau, 1981).

Politics

Fawkes, (Sir) Randol   *The Faith that Moved the Mountain* (Nassau, 1979).

Hughes, Colin   *Race and Politics in the Bahamas* (St Lucia, London 1981).

Johnson, (Dame) Doris   *The Quiet Revolution in the Bahamas* (Nassau, 1972).

Taylor, H.M.   *My Political Memoirs* (Nassau, 1987).

Customs

Bethel, Clement   Bahamian Music (including a study of Junkanoo) (M.A. Thesis, U.C.L.A., 1978).

Bethel, E. Clement (edited and expanded by Nicolette Bethel, paintings by Brent Malone)   *Junkanoo* (London, 1991).

Eneas, Cleveland   *Bain Town* (Nassau, 1973).

McCartney, T.   *Ten, Ten The Bible Ten. Obeah in the Bahamas* (Nassau, 1976).

Dialect

Holm, J. and Shilling, A.   *Dictionary of Bahamian English* (New York, 1982).

Shilling, Alison   Some Non-Standard Features of Bahamian Dialect Syntax (Ph.D. Dissertation, University of Hawaii, 1978).

Historic buildings and architecture

Douglas, Robert   *Island Heritage* (Nassau, 1992).

Public Records Office, Nassau   *A Selection of Historic Buildings in the Bahamas* (Nassau, 1975).

Russel, Sieghbert   *Nassau's Historic Buildings* (Bahamas National Trust, Nassau, 1980).

Saunders, G. and Cartwright, D.   *Historic Nassau* (London, 1979).

Social history

Craton, Michael and Saunders, Gail   *Islanders in the Stream. A History of the Bahamian People, Vol I. From Aboriginal Times to the End of Slavery* (University of Georgia Press, Athens and London, 1992).

Saunders, D. Gail   The Social History of The Bahamas (Ph.D. Thesis, University of Waterloo, Ontario, Canada, 1985).

Immigration

Johnson, Howard   'Safeguarding Our Traders: The Beginnings of Immigration Restrictions in the Bahamas, 1925 – 1933', *Immigrants and Minorities* (Vol. 5, March 1986, No 1, pp5 – 27).

Labour

Johnson, Howard   'The Share System in the Bahamas in the Nineteenth and Early Twentieth Centuries', *Slavery and Abolition* (Vol.5, No.2, Sept. 1984, pp141 – 153).

Johnson Howard   'A Modified Form of Slavery: The Credit and Truck System in the Bahamas in the Nineteenth and Early Twentieth Centuries', *Comparative Studies in Society and History* (Vol.28 No.4, Oct. 1986, pp 729 – 753).

Johnson, Howard   *The Bahamas in Slavery and Freedom* (Kingston and London, 1991).

MACMILLAN CARIBBEAN GUIDES SERIES

Dyde: *Antigua & Barbuda: The Heart of the Caribbean*
Saunders: *The Bahamas: A Family of Islands*
Hoyos: *Barbados: The Visitor's Guide*
Raine: *The Islands of Bermuda: Another World*
Cutlack: *Belize: Ecotourism in Action*
Gravette: *Cuba: Official Guide*
Halabi: *Curaçao Close-Up*
Honychurch: *Dominica: Isle of Adventure*
Sinclair: *Grenada: Isle of Spice*
Dyde: *Islands to the Windward: Five Gems of the Caribbean* (St
   Maarten/St Martin, St Barts, St Eustatius, Saba, Anguilla)
Sherlock and Preston: *Jamaica: Fairest Isle: An Introduction and
   Guide*
Fergus: *Montserrat: Emerald Isle of the Caribbean*
Gordon: *Nevis: Queen of the Caribees*
Dyde: *St Kitts: Cradle of the Caribbean*
Ellis: *St Lucia: Helen of the West Indies*
Sutty: *St Vincent and the Grenadines*
Taylor: *Trinidad and Tobago: A Guide and Introduction*
Smithers: *The Turks and Caicos Islands: Lands of Discovery*
Shepard: *The British Virgin Islands: Treasure Islands of the
   Caribbean*

OTHER BOOKS ON THE BAHAMAS FROM MACMILLAN

Albury: *The Story of the Bahamas*
Albury: *Paradise Island Story*
Barratt: *Grand Bahama – Second Edition*
Waterman: *The Bahamas, A Social Studies Course for Secondary
   Schools*
Campbell: *The Ephemeral Islands, A Natural History of the
   Bahamas*
Bahamian Anthology
Saunders: *Historic Nassau*
Saunders: *Bahamian Loyalists and Their Slaves*
Sealey: *The Bahamas Today*
Popov: *The Bahamas Rediscovered*
Riley and Lowe: *The Lucayans*
Bethel: *Junkanoo: Festival of the Bahamas*
Cash, Gordan, Saunders: *Sources of Bahamian History*